BEGINNER'S GUIDE TO

Birdwatching

P9-EJK-539

Todd A. Culver
Consultant

Paul M. Konrad
Contributing writer

PUBLICATIONS INTERNATIONAL, LTD.

Todd A. Culver, consultant, is the Education Specialist at Cornell Laboratory of Ornithology at Cornell University. He contributes to the nationally aired radio program *Birdwatch*.

Paul M. Konrad, contributing writer, is a professional ornithologist. He is currently the managing editor of *Wildbird* magazine and has written extensively on birds for scientific journals and the general audience.

TABLE OF CONTENTS

INTRODUCTION

Beyond your backyard there are some interesting birds. The spotted sandpiper is a fascinating bird that you see at a shoreline.

Birds are fascinating. Their beautiful spring songs brighten our mornings, we are awed at their effortless flight, and their vibrant colors add a pleasant diversion from our daily routines. Most importantly, birds bring us closer to the natural world around us.

For some people, this casual interest has become a quest. They are intrigued by the diversity of birds and their widely differing appearances and behaviors. These people try to attract birds to their backyards, and they search for birds in remote areas. This interest in birds has given them a hobby—birdwatching.

Over 800 different species of birds have been recorded in North America, north of the Mexican border. This is only about 9 percent of the world's 9,000 bird species. There are always new birds to see, new behaviors to witness, and new areas in which to find wild birds.

While birdwatching can be done alone, many birders enjoy sharing their experiences—so they have formed clubs. The memberships in local bird clubs cross ethnic, cultural, and national lines. Birdwatching brings people together from different backgrounds.

Birding Afield

Birdwatching involves looking for birds, identifying them, and finding out their habits and movements through observation and reading. Birds have daily activity patterns. Some birds are most active in the morning and evening hours, others are active throughout the day, and some birds are most active at night. If you know the daily rhythms of birds you wish to spot, you will make your birdwatching time more fruitful.

Birds also have seasonal and annual cycles. There is the nesting season, spring and fall migrations, and a winter season. The birds you will find in an area will depend on the season and where you are birding.

You can watch birds anywhere—in cities or remote wild regions, you can watch from your car, while on foot, or in a boat or plane. Each mode of transportation will provide a different birding experience. On foot it is best if you move slowly and listen for bird songs or their movements in plants. Also, watch for motion as they fly or make their way through ground cover. As you walk, don't let the birds know of your presence. You can even hide in natural cover or an artificial blind. It is satisfying to watch birds carry on with their normal lives.

As you gain experience, you will be able to identify a yellow warbler by its song, "sweet, sweet, sweet, I'm so sweet."

Begin Birdwatching

Sometimes you will only have a quick glance at a bird; from that you must distinguish its characteristics so you can identify it. Identifying birds becomes easier and more fun as you gain experience. To distinguish a species, look for distinctive size, shape, colors, markings, silhouette, flight pattern, behavior, and songs or calls. There is always something more to learn.

The red-headed woodpecker's range is east of the Rocky Mountains (except New York and New England).

You cannot keep all these identification clues in mind for each species you might see. You will also need a field guide. Field guides provide an illustration of the birds you may find with a range map and descriptions of some common behavior characteristics. The *Beginner's Guide To Birdwatching* provides an introduction to the birds of North America, and 100 of the most common birds are described and pictured. Your field guide is valuable for identifying new birds and verifying other birds you can identify by sight.

The most basic equipment needed for birdwatching is a pencil and a pad of paper. If you spot a bird you don't know, write down where you spotted it, its characteristics, its behavior, and anything else you notice. Then when you have time, you can go to your field guide to try and identify the bird. You also have taken notes to remember your trip by.

Binoculars are also helpful. Binoculars magnify birds seven to ten times, depending on the magnification power of the pair you choose. Spotting scopes offer more magnification, from 15 to 60 times. But you need a tripod when using a spotting scope to keep it steady.

Many birdwatchers keep lists of the birds they see. A life list is the most common. It includes all the birds a person has seen in her or his lifetime. Other lists incorporate geographic boundaries, such as a North American list or a state list. You can keep a list for a selected time period—a day list, a month list, or an annual list. You can keep a list for any reason you want, such as a list for a certain location or a special trip.

Once you progress beyond identifying birds, you will begin to study the behavior of the birds. You will marvel to see interactions between birds, watch them search for and collect food, and look into their "private" nesting behavior. These behaviors will be obvious if you watch an eastern bluebird singing its spring territorial song and displaying with a potential mate. You may later see it making feeding forays from its birdhouse, and returning with insects for its nestlings. You will find a whole world of exciting behavior!

Some birds confuse even veteran birders. Many female hummingbirds are very hard to tell apart, including this ruby-throated hummer.

Geographic Diversity

You will quickly notice that the kinds of birds you see will differ from one area to another. The diversity of birds differs with geography, the climate, the physical characteristics of the area, and the type of habitat. You will find different birds in a temperate region than you will in a tropical or arctic location.

Each species of bird has adapted to life through the process of evolution. A species is found where its specific needs, such as food, water, and breeding, are available. For instance, the great blue heron has long legs for wading in shallow water, where it hunts for fish and other small aquatic animals. In addition, it has long, widely splayed toes that help support it in muddy ground.

The eastern bluebird needs a cavity to nest in. It must compete with more aggressive cavity-nesting birds.

The great blue heron is well adapted to its way of life.

Science

The science of studying birds is ornithology, and scientists or biologists who study birds are called ornithologists. Birds are an important part of our wildlife heritage. Many professionals study birds. These professionals include wildlife biologists, land and resource managers, university professors, park and refuge personnel, wildlife writers and publishers, wildlife photographers, natural history museum biologists and taxonomists, and many others. Today, field biologists use state-of-the-art electronics to track birds, including radio telemetry, radar, and even satellite tracking equipment.

Amateur birders can also add to scientific information. Keep accurate records about unusual sightings or a given location—this can be helpful for researchers who are looking for

This wildlife biologist is checking a Canada goose's nest and eggs.

information. Your birding notes may be a gold mine of data someday! Amateurs can also participate in volunteer-based research and surveys, such as the Christmas Bird Count.

Classification Of Birds

Each bird is named and categorized by a variety of characteristics. The American Ornithologists' Union (A.O.U.) names and classifies birds in North America. This scientific group provides one common name and one two-word scientific name—a genus and a species name—for each species. The common name is English, and the scientific name is Latin. For example, the common loon is named *Gavia immer*. Common loon is its common name, *Gavia* is its genus name, and *immer* is the species portion of its name. These names distinguish this species from other species of loons.

Species are separated by size, shape, color, general behavior, song, and ecological requirements. Species are generally not capable of breeding with another species. The terms

The snow goose is related to the emperor goose, which are both members of the genus Chen.

subspecies and race are interchangeable. They are groups that are distinct, but they can interbreed. A species may have two or more subspecies, or it may have none.

Related species are grouped into a genus. Related genera (plural of genus) are incorporated into families. And related families are put into an order. All bird orders are members of one class (Aves).

Bird Biology—What is a Bird?

Birds are animals with a backbone and feathers. They are warm-blooded animals that can regulate their body temperatures separate from their surroundings. Birds have four-chambered hearts and lay eggs. For most birds, flight is their principal means of movement, although most can also walk and run; some swim, dive, or glide. Although some species have lost the ability to fly, including penguins, ostriches, and kiwis, all birds were once able to fly.

Feathers

Every bird is covered by feathers and no other animal has them. Feathers provide three very important functions: they insulate to reduce the loss of body heat, they are the physical "hardware" to fly, and they give birds their coloring.

A downy woodpecker has about 2,000 feathers. The much larger tundra swan has about 25,000 feathers.

Feathers are very strong for their size and weight. They are made of keratin, the same material in your fingernails. There are different types of feathers. Contour feathers cover the bird's body; they are smooth so the air glides over them when the bird flies. Down feathers trap air and keep the bird warm. Feathers are arranged on bird's bodies in distinct feather tracts. Areas between feather tracts may remain bare or they may be covered by down, as they are in ducks. The actual number of feathers on a bird varies. As you might expect, bigger birds usually have more feathers.

A bird's wing and tail have its largest feathers—the flight feathers. The primaries are the outermost feathers on its wings. The secondaries are the ones closer to its body—where the wing folds.

Flight

Flying is a bird's most remarkable ability. Flight may be as simple and effortless as gliding or soaring on air currents, or as difficult and strenuous as hovering or flapping against a strong wind. The flight feathers of birds, mostly the long feathers of the wings and tail, provide the maneuverability necessary for sustained accurate flight.

To develop the ability to fly, ancestral birds went through a series of adaptions to their anatomy. As a result, modern birds have light, strong feathers; light, streamlined bodies with a central point of balance; and a sternum keel where flight muscles are attached. The chest muscles that attach to the sternum are large compared to the bird's body size.

Another adaption that most birds have is that their bones are thin and hollow—making the birds very light. Also, they have large air sacs in their bodies to make them even lighter. Instead of heavy teeth, birds have a light, strong bill (also made of keratin). Engineers are amazed by nature's flying machines—birds.

Some birds can fly long distances without resting, such as snow geese, which fly 2,400 miles nonstop during migration. Other birds can fly at extraordinary speeds, including the peregrine falcon and golden eagle, both of which can exceed 200 miles per hour when they make spectacular dives at their prey.

The peregrine falcon must be able to dive quickly to catch its fast-moving prey.

Migration

In areas where freezing temperatures make food and water hard to find, birds are forced to migrate. However, the seasonally abundant food available in temperate and subarctic regions brings back many birds to breed and feed during the milder seasons. Over time, populations have adapted to these seasonal movements and each year millions of birds migrate to warmer weather in the winter and back again in the spring.

Plumage

Birds have a wide variety of plumages. Some are brightly colored, such as the painted bunting and the ring-necked pheasant. Others are camouflaged, such as sage grouse. Birds molt—they shed and replace their feathers. Most birds have at least one full molt each year, usually in late summer after their nesting season is finished. Male, female, juvenile, immature, and eclipse (nonbreeding) plumages are common among some groups of birds. Many perching birds and waterfowl have distinct male and female plumages, while most birds of prey have immature plumages.

Feeding

Many birdwatchers watch the feeding behavior of birds. Finding food and adapting to available food has been important in the evolution of birds—and one of the things that makes them such a diverse group. Birds have been successful in finding and feeding on different types of foods in different places to ensure survival, including plants, seeds, fruit, flower nectar, insects and other invertebrates, fish, amphibians, reptiles, other birds, and mammals. Some birds eat only certain foods, while others feed on a variety of foods. Hummingbirds are specialized feeders—they need flower nectar and some small insects.

Birds have special adaptions that help them to find and eat certain foods. For instance, a bird's beak, neck, legs, feet,

A hummingbird's long, thin bill allows it to get the nectar from a flower.

claws, eyes, ears, and other features may help it search for food. Specialized beaks help find, capture, and eat food. A finch uses its conical, strong, pointed bill to pick up, crack, and eat seeds. A woodpecker uses its long, hard, pointed bill to pry into bark and chisel into dead wood to find insects and their larvae. A pelican uses its membranous, pouched bill to catch fish underwater.

Reproduction

The breeding behavior of birds is fascinating. The reproductive cycle of most birds includes attracting a mate, establishing a territory, nesting, egg-laying, incubation, and the care of young. The breeding strategies of birds are nearly as diverse as birds themselves. To attract a female, males have a distinct plumage, and they use a variety of displays and songs.

The American robin uses a common bird-breeding strategy. Male robins arrive at the breeding area ahead of females and

A robin's work is never done. The nestlings constantly beg for food from their parents.

claim an area that has an adequate food supply and at least one usable nest site. The male perches on a prominent site and sings to advertise its territorial claim to other males and to attract a female. The male will repel all other male robins from the area. When a female is attracted to the site, the male displays and sings. A pair bond will be formed between the male and female that will last through the first nesting attempt and probably through the following nesting attempts that season. The male assists the female with nest building, and although the female incubates the eggs, the male assists with feeding and protecting the nestlings. In fact, the male will attend to the fledged brood while the female lays and incubates a second clutch.

Nesting

Most birds lay their eggs in nests. Nests may be intricately woven hangings like the northern oriole's hanging basket, or they may be as simple as a scrape in the soil like the killdeer's. Some birds, such as owls, do not build their own nests, but lay their eggs in natural tree cavities. The great horned owl takes over an old nest of a hawk or other large bird.

Nest-site selection is likewise diverse. Most people think of birds nesting in trees, and indeed, most birds do nest in trees. They may build their nest in the crotch of a tree branch, or in a naturally hollowed cavity. Woodpeckers drill out their own nesting cavities in dead branches, which are then used by other birds in following years. Some birds nest on an open sandy beach, preferably on an island or sandbar, like the common tern. Some birds prefer to build their nests on buildings and bridges. Actually, egg-laying can begin before the nest is completed. Upland-nesting ducks tend to add nest material during egg-laying and incubation; the females pluck down from their breast to add to the nest.

Eggs

One of the things that characterizes birds from other animals is their hard-shelled eggs (though some birds lay leathery eggs like reptiles). Female birds have a functional left ovary and oviducts where eggs are produced and fertilized by male sperm. The hard shell is made mostly of calcium. Usually one egg is laid each day until the clutch is complete. Each egg contains an embryo that is nourished during development by the yolk and albumen stored in the egg. Microscopic pores in the eggshell permit exchange of oxygen, carbon dioxide, and other gases. One or both adults cover the eggs with their bodies (one at a time), usually using the breast and belly to keep the eggs warm and incubate them.

Incubation of the eggs may start when the first egg is laid, or it may wait until the full clutch has been laid. If incubation begins immediately, the eggs will hatch in the order they are laid, a day or two apart. This will result in a hierarchy of nestlings, with the first to hatch several days older than the last. This is common among predatory birds, whose nesting success may depend on the abundance of prey. In years of plentiful food, nestling survival will be high. However, if there is inadequate prey, only the older, more aggressive nestlings will survive.

The incubation period may be rapid—11 days for some small birds like the black-capped chickadee. But it may take much longer—up to 40 days for golden eagles. When the embryo has developed, the chick uses an egg tooth on the top of its beak to break a hole in the egg (known as pipping). It begins breaking the shell with its beak, kicking with its feet, and pushing with its wings and head. The adults may help the chick. There is usually some communication between the chick and adults—peeping can sometimes be heard from inside an egg even before the egg is pipped.

The killdeer makes a scrape in the ground to lay her eggs, which look much like rocks and blend into the surroundings.

A female wood duck watches her young. These precocial young can walk and begin feeding soon after hatching.

Brood Rearing

Hatchling birds are either altricial or precocial. Altricial birds are naked and blind and remain in the nest for two weeks or longer. They are fed by one or both parents until they fledge. Precocial birds hatch with a full covering of down, they can regulate their body temperatures within hours, they can walk and follow the adults from the nest within 24 hours, and many begin feeding on their own shortly thereafter. All ducks, geese, swans, grouse, pheasants, rails, cranes, plovers, and sandpipers have precocial young. Development of young birds is rapid. American robins increase their weight by ten times between hatching and fledging.

Fledging is when a young bird first begins to fly. For altricial birds, fledging happens when the birds leave their nests. First flights may be simple gliding flights with awkward landings. Refining the ability to fly may take several days or weeks.

A male cardinal is a breathtaking sight!

The Wonder of Birds

Without question, birds have captured the interest and curiosity of people for centuries. Each year, more people begin watching birds and others become more dedicated to a pastime that knows no limits or boundaries. Enjoy the wonders of birds along with us!

A GUIDE TO THE GALLERY

The birds in this book are arranged into convenient groupings that make them easier to study and enjoy. Scientists—called taxonomists—also place birds into groups based on how closely they are related to one another. All living organisms are placed into these groups: kingdom, phylum, class, order, family, genus, and species. All birds belong to the class Aves; humans belong to the class Mammals. The scientific name given a bird is its genus and species names. Birds grouped together in the same genus are thought to have recently evolved from a common ancestor. Birds placed in different orders had a common ancestor long ago—they have had more time to evolve differently. The birds in the gallery have been placed in taxonomic order, just like most field guides. This will help you find and identify new birds. Enjoy learning about the birds as you go through this book. Then go outside and begin watching and learning even more about our feathered friends!

Waterbirds

These birds are closely tied to water. The loons and grebes are ancient birds that have remained unchanged for millions of years. Most of the birds in this group are adapted for diving. Below the water's surface, they capture fish or find aquatic plants to feed on. This group includes some of the best swimmers in the bird world.

Wading birds

Members of the heron family and the cranes make a living wading in shallow water hunting for food. They are opportunistic feeders and eat everything from fish to waste agricultural grains. Adaptations for a wading lifestyle include long thin legs, large feet perfectly suited for walking on mud, and large sharp bills that can strike out at prey like a dagger.

Waterfowl

The birds in this group are closely related. Because of their similarities, ornithologists have placed these birds in the order Anseriformes. Most swans, ducks, and geese are found in freshwater marshes, lakes, and rivers. Dabbling ducks feed in shallow water and "tip up" as they reach down into the water for food. The canvasback is a diving duck. It can swim underwater to find food on the bottom of deep-water lakes and oceans.

Birds of Prey

This group contains the orders Falconiformes (vultures, eagles, hawks, and falcons) and Strigiformes (owls). They are predators and sport strong talons, excellent eyesight, and hooked bills. These birds are perfectly suited for catching and killing prey.

The common loon is a bird that has not changed for many millions of years.

Gamebirds

These closely related birds belong to the order Galliformes. They are ground-dwelling birds that have a large storage area in their digestive systems called a crop. Gamebirds quickly fill their crops and retreat to protective cover to digest their food. All the birds in this group are hunted by sport hunters.

Shorebirds, Gulls, and Terns

This is another group in which all the birds belong to the same order—Charadriiformes. Shorebirds can be found probing the beaches and mud flats for food, especially at low tide. Some shorebirds, such as the killdeer and American woodcock, are found in upland areas. Gulls and terns are a diverse group closely related to shorebirds. Gulls and terns share the seashore habitats with shorebirds.

The beautiful ring-necked pheasant is a commonly hunted bird.

Perching Birds

Perching birds belong to the order Passeriformes, the largest and most advanced group of birds. Most of the birds in this group are songbirds—known to bird-watchers for their beautiful and complex songs. One of the greatest challenges in birding is to learn to recognize the many warblers by sight and by their songs. Most of these birds migrate—traveling north to breed and raise their young and spending winters in southern tropical forests. Ornithologists are concerned that many of the most spectacular species are declining due to rainforest deforestation and the development and fragmentation of North American forests.

Maps

The maps are provided to give you an idea of each bird's range—where it may be found. Some species do not migrate, but other species migrate from northern to southern regions. We have provided the birds' summer, winter, and year-long ranges, where appropriate. These maps are based on current information, but many species contract and expand their ranges over time.

The peregrine falcon's sharp, hooked beak gives us a clue that it is a bird of prey.

Landbirds

This group is really a mixed bag. The birds in this group belong to several different orders and are not closely related. They are fascinating because of their wonderful diversity. Birds such as woodpeckers, hummingbirds, cuckoos, and swifts are perfectly suited to their particular lifestyles. From the woodpecker's chisellike bill and grasping feet to the intricacy of the hummingbird's tongue—there are many interesting things to learn about these birds.

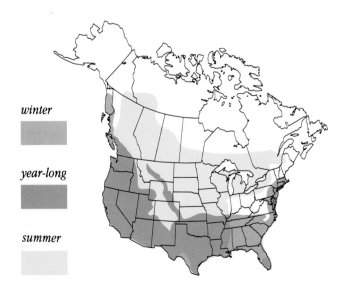

winter

year-long

summer

COMMON LOON
Gavia immer

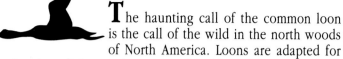

Common loon; **group:** waterbird; **family:** loon.

The haunting call of the common loon is the call of the wild in the north woods of North America. Loons are adapted for swimming, diving, and catching fish. Their legs are far back on their bodies, and their webbed feet help them swim and dive. Loons have strong, thick beaks for catching small fish, and they can dive more than 600 feet below the water's surface.

Common loons cannot stand, so their nesting sites must be where they can push themselves onto land. The nest site is usually along the shoreline of an island in a freshwater lake. The parents also choose a place that can provide a "nursery" pool. The water should be clear and free from predators, and have enough fish to feed the loon chicks for 11 weeks. This is where the chicks learn to dive and fish for food. Loon chicks can swim two days after hatching!

NESTING: Pair shares incubation and brood rearing. Clutch of 2 olive (brown-marked) eggs hatches in about 4 weeks. Chicks fledge in about 11 weeks.

PLUMAGE: During breeding season, black and iridescent-green head and neck, black and white back and wings, and white breast and belly. In winter, gray brown above and white below. It has a black bill.

SIZE: 32 inches.

CALL: A yodeling three-syllable call.

HABITAT: Freshwater lakes in forests during breeding season and ocean coastlines and the Great Lakes in winter.

Watching the intimate courtship display of western grebes is a high point for any birdwatcher. The pair exchanges food, bobs their heads, and offers nesting material to one another. Then suddenly, they burst from the water with their bodies held upright, heads held high, and their long necks slightly bent. They rush forward in a dancelike display as they run across the water.

Western grebes eat fish and other animals that live in water, which they catch while diving below the water's surface. Grebe chicks often ride high and dry on the backs of their father or mother. The young are fed feathers by the adults— the adults eat them too! The feathers ball in their stomachs and protect them from sharp fish bones. The feathers also slow their digestion so that bones can dissolve without harming the birds.

NESTING: Pair incubates the 3 bluish-white eggs for 23 days. Chicks fledge in 9 to 11 weeks.

PLUMAGE: Black above and white below. The black coloring on the face extends below their red eyes.

SIZE: 25 inches.

CALL: Loud "*kreek-kreek.*"

HABITAT: Shallow inland wetlands, lakes, and rivers during the breeding season, and ocean coastlines and inland lakes during the winter.

WESTERN GREBE
Aechmophorus occidentalis

Western grebe; **group:** waterbird; **family:** grebe.

AMERICAN WHITE PELICAN

Pelecanus erythrorhynchos

American white pelican; **group:** *waterbird;* **family:** *pelican.*

Imagine opening your mouth and having a ready-made fishnet. That is almost what the American white pelican has. Its expandable throat pouch can hold up to three gallons of water! The pelican uses its pouch to capture and hold fish and other food it finds in the water. It is a bird that is well-suited to living along the water, with its webbed feet and pouched bill. White pelicans may feed in groups—they herd the fish into an area where they are easier to catch. They also swim alone, submerging their heads to hunt for fish. Pelicans also eat salamanders and crayfish during the summer. White pelicans seem a bit ungainly on land, but they are beautiful birds in flight.

American white pelicans nest in large breeding colonies—there may be as many as 5,000 nesting pairs on islands in inland lakes. A pelican clutch is two eggs. Unfortunately, both chicks do not always survive. The second chick is usually killed by its larger sibling or it starves. But the surviving pelican is hardy. At nine weeks old, it can have eaten up to 150 pounds of fish brought to it by its parents!

NESTING: Pair incubates clutch of 2 eggs, which hatches in 29 to 36 days. Both brood chicks, which fledge in 8 to 9 weeks.

PLUMAGE: White plumage with black primary and secondary flight feathers. Bill and feet are orange.

SIZE: 62 inches.

HABITAT: Coastal lakes, marshes, saltwater bays, beaches.

BROWN PELICAN

Pelecanus occidentalis

Though it is not graceful as it takes off, a flock of brown pelicans in flight is a lovely sight. As a pelican flies along an ocean coastline on wings that span almost seven feet, it can spy prey in the water below. It whirls into a beak-first dive after a school of small fish and catches a fish in the expandable pouch of its lower bill. It then tips its bill down to drain the water, and tips it up to swallow the fish. Sometimes the pelican is caught off guard and a gull will snatch the fish from its very mouth. Brown pelicans are rarely seen away from warm ocean coastlines. They feed almost entirely on fish.

Brown pelicans were placed on the endangered species list in the 1960s. They lost some of their habitat to humans, and DDT caused thinning of their eggshells. Though the populations are increasing, it will take a while for a full recovery.

NESTING: Pair nests on ground or in mangrove trees. Both incubate the 3 white eggs, which hatch in about 30 days. Nestling period may extend up to 12 weeks.

PLUMAGE: Mostly brown gray with a white head and neck, and yellow crown. Breeding adult has red-brown nape.

SIZE: 48 inches.

CALL: Adults mostly silent.

HABITAT: Warm ocean coastal areas.

Brown pelican; **group:** *waterbird;* **family:** *pelican.*

American coots are known for their habit of running along the top of the water's surface with wings flapping, as though they were too heavy to become airborne. But this is their usual mode of flying. Coots are very territorial, and neighboring males often fight, which provides a flurry of activity in shallow wetlands. Some fights become violent, with the coots biting and clawing one another until one flees in typical coot fashion—skittering over the water's surface.

American coots have lobed feet. Their feet help them swim, and the sharp claws at the end of their talons are dangerous weapons. But their feet have another interesting use—they conduct heat from the body, which cools the bird off.

American coots eat plants and animals that live in the water. Coots carry their young on their back, and when the coot dives for food, the young hold on to the back feathers of the parent with their bills. Is this the coot equivalent of a ride at an amusement park?

AMERICAN COOT
Fulica americana

American coot; **group:** waterbird; **family:** coots, gallinules, and rails.

NESTING: Clutch of 8 to 12 light-pink eggs hatches in 21 to 25 days. Chicks fledge in 7 to 8 weeks.

PLUMAGE: Dark gray; with a black head, neck, and tail.

SIZE: 15 inches.

CALL: *"Kuk-kuk-kuk-kuk."*

HABITAT: Freshwater lakes, ponds, marshes, and rivers.

DOUBLE-CRESTED CORMORANT
Phalacrocorax auritus

Double-crested cormorant; **group:** waterbird; **family:** cormorant.

Double-crested cormorants may be mistaken for geese as they fly in V-formation, but when they land there is no question that cormorants are masters of the water. One reason is that they can see equally well underwater as above. They are among the best divers and are adept at capturing fish, their main food. Besides fish, cormorants feed on salamanders and invertebrates that live in water. Cormorants regurgitate indigestible objects in pellet form, just like owls.

Double-crested cormorants have complex courtship displays. Males chase the females and splash forcefully with both wings. The males then swim in a zigzag pattern and submerge their heads. They then dive and surface holding vegetation. Males drop the vegetation near the females or toss the plants into the air. Breeding pairs nest in colonies on islands or in the bare branches of flooded dead trees. Tree nests are usually large and built with sticks.

NESTING: Pair shares incubation of the 3 or 4 light-blue eggs for 25 to 29 days. Nestlings fledge in 5 to 6 weeks.

PLUMAGE: Black with a small orange throat patch.

SIZE: 32 inches.

CALL: A grunt that sounds a bit piglike.

HABITAT: Along ocean coastlines, inland lakes, and rivers.

ATLANTIC PUFFIN
Fratercula arctica

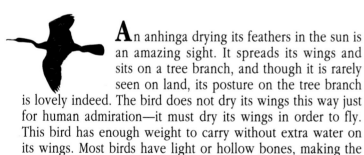

Atlantic puffin; **group:** *waterbird;* **family:** *auk.*

The comical-looking Atlantic puffin is a favorite bird, even though few people ever see them except in a zoo. The puffin's broad, colorful beak and bright-orange webbed feet give it a clownlike appearance, but in fact this seabird is not built for comedy. It is built for its diving and fishing life at sea, where it may dive up to 100 feet deep for food. And there is nothing funny about the serious decline of the puffin population since the 1800s. Some people were collecting their eggs and hunting the birds for commercial purposes. But recently the birds have been reintroduced to islands off the coast of Maine—so there is hope for the puffin's future.

The lovely bill of the Atlantic puffin takes a while to form; it may take a young puffin up to five years to get its full-size bill. The puffin's bill is important in breeding displays; it attracts a mate. Before breeding season begins, the puffin's bill develops bright plates. These later drop off after they mate. A puffin's favorite foods include fish, squid, shrimp, and other small animals that live in the ocean.

NESTING: Pair incubates the 1 white egg, which is laid in sandy soil or a rocky crevice. Egg hatches in 40 to 45 days, and chicks fledge in 5 to 6 weeks.

PLUMAGE: Mostly black with a white face, breast, and belly.

SIZE: 12 inches.

HABITAT: North Atlantic Ocean.

ANHINGA
Anhinga anhinga

An anhinga drying its feathers in the sun is an amazing sight. It spreads its wings and sits on a tree branch, and though it is rarely seen on land, its posture on the tree branch is lovely indeed. The bird does not dry its wings this way just for human admiration—it must dry its wings in order to fly. This bird has enough weight to carry without extra water on its wings. Most birds have light or hollow bones, making the bird lightweight and helping it fly. But an anhinga is built for diving and has solid bones. For a bird, it is quite heavy.

The anhinga spears a fish or frog with its long, sharp bill while swimming below the water's surface. On the surface, it tosses the fish or frog in the air and swallows it. This bird has very wettable feathers. That means it can control its buoyancy—it can sink effortlessly into water. Most water birds would quickly bob to the surface if they tried to dive like the anhinga. It is found in tropical swamps and freshwater wetlands in the southeastern United States.

Anhinga; **group:** *waterbird;* **family:** *snakebird.*

NESTING: Pair builds nest of sticks and twigs in a tree next to water. Clutch of 4 white eggs hatches in about 4 weeks. Fledging time unknown.

PLUMAGE: Mostly black with white streaks on the upper wing feathers.

SIZE: 35 inches.

HABITAT: Tropical freshwater wetlands.

AMERICAN BITTERN
Botaurus lentiginosus

*American bittern; **group:** wading bird; **family:** heron and bittern.*

The American bittern is a master of disguise. It lives in thick wetland vegetation, where it is hidden among the reeds and cattails by its drab, brown-streaked plumage. But this bird takes camouflage one step further—it can stay motionless with its neck stretched upward and its bill pointed at the sky. With its vertically lined breast plumage, it blends in as another clump of reeds. Even though these shy birds are rarely spotted, you can locate them by their songs, which fill marshlands with a pumping sound—not unlike water chugging from a jug. The American bittern eats fish, frogs, salamanders, insects, and other small invertebrates.

The American bittern population has been declining. It has lost much of its habitat—the wetlands—to human development. And the redhead (a diving duck) does not help the situation. It will sometimes dump its egg in a bittern's nest, which puts the bittern young in danger when the eggs hatch (the duckling often kills the bittern young).

NESTING: Female builds nest and incubates the 4 or 5 buff-colored eggs, which hatch in about 4 weeks. Fledging time unknown.

PLUMAGE: Shades of brown with a mostly tan breast and a black line on both sides of the neck.

SIZE: 28 inches.

SONG: A slow, deep *"oong ka-choonk, oong ka-choonk, oong ka-choonk."*

HABITAT: Thick emergent wetland vegetation.

GREAT BLUE HERON
Ardea herodias

*Great blue heron; **group:** wading bird; **family:** heron and bittern.*

Standing almost four feet tall with wings that span six feet, the great blue heron is one of the tallest North American birds. Its long legs, neck, and bill also distinguish this common wading bird. The best place to find great blue herons is in shallow water, where they catch and eat small fish, crayfish, frogs, and snakes. An amazing thing about herons is that the older they get, the better fishers they become. Adults are about two times better at fishing than younger birds. Practice makes perfect in the bird world!

Great blue heron nestlings must be protected from many dangers if they are to grow up and become adult birds. But these nestlings face a unique danger—turkey vultures. The vulture forces the nestling to regurgitate its last meal, which the vulture scoops up. That then becomes a meal for the vulture chicks!

NESTING: Pair incubates the 5 blue-green eggs for 28 days. Nestlings fledge in about 8 weeks.

PLUMAGE: Gray blue overall with a white face, yellow bill, black stripe across the crown, and black flight feathers. During breeding season, adults have ornate plumes.

SIZE: 48 inches.

CALL: Adult bellows hoarse squawks when alarmed.

HABITAT: Freshwater and brackish marshes, swamps, lakes, rivers, and mangroves.

GREAT EGRET
Casmerodius albus

Few birds rival the elegance of a great egret in flight, with its pure-white plumage and the graceful, sweeping strokes of its broad wings. This tall, beautiful wading bird is also an amazing hunter. It stalks through shallow water on its long black legs in search of fish and other small animals that it snatches with its long yellow beak. But it is even better at something else—stealing! The great egret occasionally steals fish from smaller herons. Studies show that the bird is five times more efficient at stealing than fishing. Maybe crime does pay—if you're a great egret!

Great egrets were in danger of becoming extinct in the 1800s because hunters were killing them for their feathers. Fashionable women wore egret feathers on their hats until concerned people stopped the killings. In fact, the National Audubon Society was organized to stop plume hunting. Until 1991, the egret was its symbol.

NESTING: Pair incubates the 3 light-blue eggs for 23 to 26 days. Young leave nest at 3 weeks, fledge in another 3 weeks.

PLUMAGE: White with black legs and a yellow bill. During breeding season, adults grow long white plumes for breeding displays, and the bare skin between their bill and eyes turns green.

SIZE: 39 inches.

HABITAT: Shallow wetlands and mud flats.

Great egret; **group:** *wading bird;* **family:** *heron and bittern.*

SANDHILL CRANE
Grus canadensis

The ancient calls of sandhill cranes trumpet through the still morning. Flock after flock arrive and land in a harvested grain field and an adjoining wet meadow grassland. They feed on waste grains in the field and earthworms in the wet meadow. Sandhill cranes also feed on insects and small aquatic animals in shallow water. During migration and in winter, thousands of sandhill cranes roost together in shallow wetlands and fly out in flocks to feed during the morning and afternoon.

Sandhill cranes are endangered. They are losing their habitat because of wetland drainage, and they are losing critical migratory stops. The Platte River, one of those migratory stops, is being diverted for crop irrigation and drinking water. Either we lose the sandhill cranes or we leave some water in the river. There is a chance to correct the damage before it's too late.

NESTING: Pair incubates the 2 tan (brown-spotted) eggs, which hatch in 28 to 32 days. Chicks fledge in about 2 months.

PLUMAGE: Gray plumage that may be stained a rusty red by iron-rich soil.

SIZE: Varies between races, but greater sandhill cranes stand about four feet tall.

CALL: A loud resonant "*garoo-gar-oo,*" that carries for more than a mile.

HABITAT: Shallow wetlands.

Sandhill crane; **group:** *wading bird;* **family:** *crane.*

WHOOPING CRANE
Grus americana

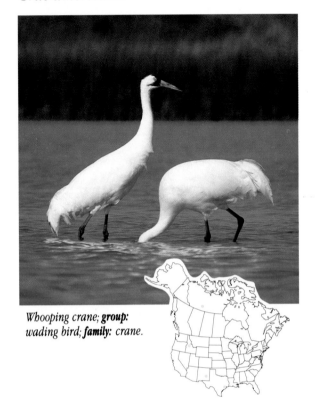

*Whooping crane; **group:** wading bird; **family:** crane.*

The whooping crane is the tallest bird in North America; it stands five feet tall! It is even more impressive in flight—with a wingspan of over seven feet. But the most spectacular feature of the crane family is its elegant courtship dance. It is so impressive that it has been imitated in the dances of African tribes, Australian Aborigines, and Native Americans. The dance can be performed by single birds, breeding pairs, groups of males only or females only, or groups of males and females. The birds walk around each other with their wings partly spread, while they bow and bob their heads. They jump in the air, and occasionally throw pieces of plants or twigs in the air, which they catch or stab when they fall. Whooping cranes feed on aquatic animals, plants, and waste grain.

Whooping cranes have inhabited the continent for millions of years, but were nearly lost when 15 remained in 1941. Today there are over 150 wild birds, but they are still on the brink of extinction.

NESTING: Pair incubates the 2 tan-spotted eggs for 30 days. Only 1 chick usually lives. Pair cares for chick about 10 months.

PLUMAGE: White with black primary wing feathers, a bare scarlet facial mask, black legs, and olive bill.

SIZE: 5 feet.

CALL: A shrill trumpeting call, "*ker-loo, ker-lee-loo.*"

HABITAT: Open wetlands.

WHITE-FACED IBIS
Plegadis chihi

To be sure you're watching an ibis, look for its long, down-curved bill. White-faced ibis are the most widespread of the three ibis species that live in North America. Ibis are medium-size wading birds that are usually found in the shallow waters of freshwater marshes searching for food with their bills. They feed mainly on fish and small aquatic invertebrates, including crayfish, shrimp, worms, and insects.

As with many other wetland species, white-faced ibis populations are declining due to human intervention in nature. Much of their wetland habitat is being drained.

White-faced ibis nest in small colonies. The breeding pair constantly guards the nest, with the female guarding it at night and the male guarding it by day. When switching places on the nest, they have an elaborate relief ceremony. The pair rattles their bills together and preens one another, while cooing.

*White-faced ibis; **group:** wading bird; **family:** ibis and spoonbill.*

NESTING: Pair builds nest and incubates the 3 or 4 green-blue eggs about 3 weeks. Nestlings fledge in 4 to 5 weeks.

PLUMAGE: Chestnut-maroon body, white facial feathers border eyes and bill. Iridescent green and violet wings and head, reddish bill, and red eyes.

SIZE: 23 inches.

HABITAT: Freshwater wetlands.

ROSEATE SPOONBILL
Ajaia ajaja

A small flock of wading birds flies across the swamp—a beautiful pink against the blue sky and water. Birders in the Gulf states often claim the roseate spoonbill as their favorite bird. It is hard to confuse it with other birds with its bright-pink color, large size, and unusual spatulate bill. Its beautiful plumage contrasts with its featherless face. These unique birds are usually seen in small flocks that wade in shallow water and feed on a variety of small aquatic invertebrates and fish.

You may not see many roseate spoonbills in your local zoo—they are very expensive to keep. If they are not fed shrimp or crayfish (very expensive foods) they lose their pink color!

In the 1800s, spoonbill populations decreased drastically because plume hunters shot the birds for their wings—which were put on ladies' hats. Today the threat to this bird is different, but may be more damaging. Wetlands, the spoonbill's habitat, are being drained for real estate development.

NESTING: Pair incubates the 3 white (brown-marked) eggs for 22 to 23 days. Nestlings fledge in 5 to 6 weeks.

PLUMAGE: White neck, breast, and upper back; pink wings, back, and tail; and red wing and rump patches.

SIZE: 32 inches.

CALL: Grunts while hunting.

HABITAT: Shallow wetlands.

Roseate spoonbill; **group:** *wading bird;* **family:** *ibis and spoonbill.*

WOOD STORK
Mycteria americana

A flock of large white birds with black flight feathers, black tails and heads circles overhead with their long legs trailing. The wood storks then glide down to a muddy island and land with braking wingbeats. Almost immediately they begin wading in the water and immerse their partly open bills. They walk along slowly, searching for fish or other prey. When their bills touch prey, a rapid bill-snap reflex is triggered. This bird does not need to locate its prey by sight!

Wood storks nest in colonies in cypress swamps. The colony may include several hundred nesting pairs of storks, along with great egrets and great blue herons. Wood storks are very sensitive to changes in water level. They nest during the dry season, when low water concentrates the fish into the deepest pools. If it rains during nesting season or if food is scarce, then the colony stops breeding.

Wood stork; **group:** *wading bird;* **family:** *stork.*

NESTING: Pair builds nest, incubates, and broods young. Clutch of 3 white eggs hatches in 28 to 32 days. Nestlings fledge in about 8 weeks.

PLUMAGE: White with black tail and flight feathers, and a bare black head and upper neck. Juveniles have feathered heads.

SIZE: 40 inches.

CALL: Adults usually silent.

HABITAT: Shallow swamps and coastal wetlands.

TUNDRA SWAN
Cygnus columbianus

Few sights compare to a flock of tundra swans flying across a cloudless sky. These large white birds are a beautiful sight in flight. But they are also quite lovely gliding along in the water. The most common swan found in the Western Hemisphere, this species was once known as the whistling swan. Tundra swans feed on underwater plants, but some wintering populations feed in agricultural areas, especially surrounding the Chesapeake Bay.

Humans love to romanticize—and the swan is the perfect bird for that. Not only are swans lovely and graceful, but they also mate for life. What better bird to personify than the swan—proof is the enduring ballet classic *Swan Lake.* Tundra swans also form a close family group. Even though the female does most of the incubation of the eggs, the male stands guard and defends his family. The cygnets are able to follow the adults soon after hatching, but they need their parents for protection and feeding.

Tundra swan; **group:** *waterfowl;* **family:** *waterfowl.*

NESTING: Pair builds nest of heaped vegetation on elevated site. Clutch of 4 or 5 cream-white eggs hatches in 35 to 40 days. Nestlings fledge in 9 to 10 weeks.

PLUMAGE: All feathers are white. Beak, legs, and webbed feet are black. Immature birds have light-gray plumage.

SIZE: 52 inches.

CALL: A mournful *"hoop, hoop."*

HABITAT: Open wetlands.

SNOW GOOSE
Chen caerulescens

A flock of snow geese is one of the most spectacular sights in North America. Tens of thousands of snow geese flock together at wintering areas and migration stops. Snow geese may form mixed flocks with Canada and white-fronted geese on their way from the arctic to the southern United States and Mexico during migration. A migrating flock may fly very high—over 10,000 feet!

At one time, the white and blue color phases of snow geese were considered two separate species. The "blue goose" is rarely seen in western populations. But scientists have grouped both together as the same species. Snow geese feed on aquatic plants, shoots, roots, tubers, and waste grain in agricultural fields.

Snow goose; **group:** *waterfowl;* **family:** *waterfowl.*

NESTING: Clutch of 3 to 5 white eggs hatches in about 24 days. Pair broods goslings, which fledge in about 7 weeks.

PLUMAGE: White-phase snow geese have white plumage with black primary feathers. The blue color phase has a white head, neck, and rump; gray-blue body and tail; and black primary and secondary wing feathers. In both, the bills, legs, and feet are pink.

SIZE: 28 inches.

CALL: A high-pitched yelp: *"ou, ou, ou."*

HABITAT: Wetlands and agricultural areas.

CANADA GOOSE
Branta canadensis

Canada goose; **group:** *waterfowl;* **family:** *waterfowl.*

The perfect autumn scene includes a V-shaped skein of Canada geese flying above a river lined with red- and gold-leafed trees. The birds' loud honking calls provide wild goose music on a crisp October day. Ornithologists think geese fly in V-formation to stay in contact with each other and to avoid collisions. They do not "draft" behind the leader as commonly thought.

There are over 30 races of Canada geese. Each race, or subspecies, is distinguished by its size, coloring, and range. Canada geese graze on green grasses and plants, or feed on waste grains and small aquatic animals.

The female Canada goose performs nesting work and incubation. The gander guards the nest site. The newly hatched goslings seem to be born with a survival instinct. Even their first day in the water they can swim up to five yards under water to hide or to get away from danger!

NESTING: Female builds nest and incubates the 4 to 7 white eggs, which hatch in 25 to 30 days. Goslings fledge in 6 to 9 weeks.

PLUMAGE: Medium brown above, light tan below, black head and neck, and white cheek patches.

SIZE: Variable between many races, from giant (45 inches) to lesser (25 inches).

CALL: *"Honk-abonk."*

HABITAT: Freshwater wetlands, lakes, and ponds.

WOOD DUCK
Aix sponsa

Wood duck; **group:** *waterfowl;* **family:** *waterfowl.*

This duck was well named. It lives on wooded rivers and ponds, and often perches on tree branches. The colorful male is one of the most beautiful North American birds. Both the male and female have distinctive crests on their heads and iridescent wing specula. To identify this duck, look for its long, squared tail; crested head; and white belly. When the wood duck flies, you can often hear its distinctive *"oo-eek"* call. Wood ducks eat plants and small animals that live in water, as well as seeds and acorns.

Wood ducks nest in nest boxes and tree cavities up to 65 feet aboveground. But this can make it a bit intimidating for a just-hatched duckling! The day after hatching, the young make spectacular jumps to the ground or water below to join their mother. They then begin their life on the water.

NESTING: Female builds nest with down from her breast. Clutch of 8 to 14 white eggs hatches in 28 to 33 days. Ducklings fledge in 7 to 9 weeks.

PLUMAGE: The male has a green head, white throat and crest lines, red eyes, chestnut breast with white spots, tan flanks, and blue-black back, wings, and tail. The female is gray brown with white spotting on the breast and a white throat and eye ring.

SIZE: 18-19 inches.

CALL: The female is most vocal with a high-pitched *"oo-eek."*

HABITAT: Wetlands surrounded by woods.

The mallard is one of the most widespread and common ducks in the Northern Hemisphere. Most Americans and Canadians can identify the green-headed male. Like many other ducks, the female is a cryptic mottled-brown bird. Her coloring helps her hide while she incubates the eggs in her ground nest. This is especially important because many mallard nests are destroyed by predators before the eggs hatch, and some females are killed while they incubate. Another danger mallards face are lead pellets left by hunters. Eating one pellet can cause lethal lead poisoning!

Mallards are members of a group of birds called puddle ducks—because they prefer shallow water. When they feed, they go headfirst into the water, and their tails stand straight up. Mallards feed on green plants, seeds (including aquatic plant seeds), waste agricultural grains, and aquatic invertebrates.

MALLARD
Anas platyrhynchos

Mallard; **group:** *waterfowl;* **family:** *waterfowl.*

NESTING: Female incubates the 7 to 10 cream eggs about 28 days. Ducklings fledge in 42 to 60 days.

PLUMAGE: Breeding males have iridescent green heads; thin, white neck rings; chestnut breasts; white bellies; gray backs and wings; black rumps; and white tails. The female is mottled brown. The male resembles the female in eclipse and juvenile plumages.

SIZE: 23 inches.

CALL: "*Quack-quack,*" by female only.

HABITAT: Interior wetlands.

NORTHERN PINTAIL

Anas acuta

Northern pintail; **group:** *waterfowl;* **family:** *waterfowl.*

Whistling wings overhead draw your eyes upward, where you behold a V-shaped flock of large, streamlined ducks. Then the flock brakes with their wings and tails and they seem to fall through the air as they make a smooth, steep descent toward the water. Once the northern pintails land, the sexes of the birds are easy to tell apart. The ducks settle into pairs with the handsome gray, white, and brown drakes—their long, black pintails held high—pressing near their sleek tan mates. They feed on seeds, aquatic vegetation, waste grains, and aquatic invertebrates.

The nesting behavior of the northern pintail is similar to other upland-nesting ducks, but the hen often selects a location that is farther from water and in sparser grass cover. She usually chooses heavily grazed pastures or stubble fields. The female pintail will feign injury to distract predators if her young are in danger.

NESTING: Female incubates the 6 to 9 olive-green or olive-buff eggs about 23 days. Ducklings fledge in 5 to 8 weeks.

PLUMAGE: The hen is tan. The male has a dark-brown head, white neck and breast, gray back and wings, a black rump, and long central tail feathers.

SIZE: 25 inches.

CALL: A high-pitched whistle.

HABITAT: Freshwater inland wetlands.

The quick, twisting flight of the blue-winged teal is thrilling to watch, but hard to follow with binoculars. These fast-paced ducks fly in and suddenly coast to a wet halt as they land on the water in pairs or small flocks. Teal antics are interesting to watch, especially during the breeding season when the males guard their territory and chase other males away from their section of a marsh. Blue-winged teals feed on aquatic plants, seeds, small animals, and insect larvae. They feed by sifting food with their specialized bills.

Cryptically colored hens nest in grass- or clover-covered uplands. The female lays 8 to 11 white eggs, which she incubates for 24 days. She begins adding down plucked from her breast to the nest near the end of incubation. The ducklings follow the female to water after hatching, where they begin feeding on microscopic shrimplike animals and mosquito larvae.

BLUE-WINGED TEAL
Anas discors

Blue-winged teal; **group:** *waterfowl;* **family:** *waterfowl.*

NESTING: Female incubates the 8 to 11 white eggs, which hatch in 24 days. Ducklings fledge in 5 to 6 weeks.

PLUMAGE: Breeding males have a blue-gray head with a white crescent on each side of the face. Pale-blue wing patches are distinctive in flight.

SIZE: 15 inches.

CALL: Females have a series of descending quacks, and males have a quiet, nasal whistle.

HABITAT: Marshes, ponds, lakes, and sluggish streams.

CINNAMON TEAL
Anas cyanoptera

Cinnamon teal; **group:** *waterfowl;* **family:** *waterfowl.*

The bright chestnut-red color of the male cinnamon teal is a beautiful sight in a quiet marsh. Just like most other hen ducks, the female is a drab brown. Lively mating flights may take place over marshlands in the spring, with several males vying for the attention of a single female. As many as six colorful males may be seen chasing the female on a twisting, rapid flight. The hen leads the males on a wild, follow-the-leader flight that is interrupted when the hen lands on water, and the males barrel into the water behind her. Then the males begin chasing one another away and bobbing their heads up and down to entice the female. Soon she takes to the air, and the flight chase begins again.

As with most ducks, the female does all nesting and brood-rearing. Redheads, mallards, and ruddy ducks often lay their eggs in the nest of a cinnamon teal—they count on the hen teal not noticing and raising their young. Maybe in a big family—7 to 12 ducklings—one more doesn't matter!

NESTING: Female incubates the 7 to 12 pale pink-buff eggs, which hatch in 21 to 25 days. Ducklings fledge in about 7 weeks.

PLUMAGE: The breeding plumage of the male is bright chestnut-red with pale-blue wing patches. Hens are drab, mottled brown with pale-blue wing patches.

SIZE: 16 inches.

HABITAT: Shallow wetlands, especially alkaline marshes.

The American wigeon is a common North American duck. Its breeding displays and nuptial flights can be quite a sight if you visit its wintering areas. During breeding season, wigeons will mix with a variety of other waterfowl. The American wigeon will flock with diving ducks that can dive in deep water to get wild celery. The wigeon steals a few strands from the diving duck when it comes out of the water. The wigeon pays the duck for its food by sending out an alarm when danger approaches. The American wigeon eats a variety of plants and animals that live in the water, including small mollusks. It will also graze on land plants and waste grain.

The female lays an egg per day in a scrape in a grass-covered nesting site. The breeding pair stays together only for the first or second week of incubation. The female does not begin incubating the eggs until she has laid a full clutch, so the chicks are born about the same time.

AMERICAN WIGEON
Anas americana

*American wigeon; **group:** waterfowl; **family:** waterfowl.*

NESTING: Female incubates the 7 to 10 eggs, which hatch in 24 days. Ducklings fledge in about 6 weeks.

PLUMAGE: The male has a white head, a green patch that extends from each eye, cinnamon breast and flanks, and white wing patches. Females are mottled brown with mottled-cinnamon flanks.

SIZE: 19 inches.

CALL: A wheezing whistle.

HABITAT: Freshwater marshes and lakes.

CANVASBACK
Aythya valisineria

*Canvasback; **group:** waterfowl; **family:** waterfowl.*

Canvasbacks are the largest North American diving ducks, but their populations have been declining. Many lakes, ponds, and marshes have been drained to water crops. This has been a problem for canvasback populations. Canvasbacks need water because they dive below the water to eat aquatic plants and small clams. Because they dive to the bottom to get food, they have also been known to ingest lead shot left by hunters. This is dangerous because only one pellet can cause lead poisoning and death.

Canvasbacks take a running start to fly rather than jumping off the water like puddle ducks. And once they do take off, watch out! They are among the fastest-flying waterfowl. Canvasbacks have been clocked at up to 70 miles per hour.

NESTING: Hen builds nest and incubates the 7 to 9 eggs, which hatch in 24 to 29 days. Ducklings fledge in 8 to 9 weeks.

PLUMAGE: The drake has a red-maroon head, black breast and tail, white belly, and white-gray back and wings.

SIZE: 21 inches.

CALL: Adults normally silent.

HABITAT: Open freshwater marshes, ponds, lakes, rivers, and bays bordered by emergent vegetation.

TURKEY VULTURE
Cathartes aura

Turkey vulture; **group:** *bird of prey;* **family:** *New World vulture.*

Few birds use the rising thermal air currents and winds as well as a turkey vulture. On a hot dry day, it can cover many square miles without even a flap of its wings. A vulture soars in search of food while expending little energy. With its six-foot wingspan, it is quite beautiful when it soars.

Turkey vultures have keen eyesight, but they can locate food—decomposing animals—by smell alone. In fact, turkey vultures have such a good sense of smell that engineers working on the Alaska pipeline have added odor to the gas so that vultures can help them find leaks! The vulture is nature's trash collector. It eats carrion—dead animals—and seldom kills its own prey. And these meals can be very messy—it will often eat even long-dead animals. The turkey vulture's naked head is well-suited for the way this bird eats.

Never approach a turkey vulture's nest. The vulture will vomit on you, and the vomit contains acids strong enough to dissolve bone. Rock climbers beware!

NESTING: Pair incubates the 2 white eggs about 40 days. Nestlings fledge in 10 to 12 weeks.

PLUMAGE: Dark brown overall with gray flight feathers. Adults have a bare pink head, neck, feet, and legs.

SIZE: 27 inches.

HABITAT: Open country, often near mountains, cliffs, or hills.

BALD EAGLE
Haliaeetus leucocephalus

This majestic bird is the national symbol of the United States of America. The bald eagle is a large, spectacular bird of prey that flies on wings that span over seven feet. Ben Franklin opposed bald eagles as our national symbol because he thought they had "bad character." Bald eagles steal fish from osprey and eat carrion (dead animals). Despite its reputation, bald eagles do fish for themselves. They dive and pluck fish from beneath the water with their large talons. They also eat small animals and waterfowl.

The bald eagle's most impressive aerial display is its diving courtship flight. A diving pair locks talons in midair and spirals downward with spread wings, only to resume their circling courtship flight moments later. Interestingly, some people have decided the eagle's scream is not as fierce as the bird looks. On television the bald eagle may have the scream of a red-tailed hawk substituted—the wonders of Hollywood!

NESTING: Pair incubates the 2 white eggs, which hatch in about 35 days. Nestlings fledge in 10 to 13 weeks.

PLUMAGE: Adults are dark brown with a bright-white head and tail.

Immature eagles are dark brown with some white feathering.

SIZE: 32-37 inches.

CALL: *"Keer-kee-kee-kee-kee."*

HABITAT: Wetlands (lakes, rivers, or oceans) bordered by forests.

Bald eagle; **group:** *bird of prey;* **family:** *hawk.*

GOLDEN EAGLE
Aquila chrysaetos

Golden eagle; **group:** bird of prey; **family:** hawk.

As the regal golden eagle soars overhead on wings spread more than seven feet wide, its size alone is impressive. But when it sights a jackrabbit on the ground below, this bird of prey folds its wings and dives at an incredible speed. It has been nicknamed the "king of birds." Like most birds of prey, the female golden eagle is larger than the male. The smaller male hunts squirrels and prairie dogs, while the female hunts jackrabbits. They may also feed on other small mammals, birds, snakes, and carrion during the winter.

Golden eagles nest on cliff ledges or in trees where a pair builds a large nest of sticks. They add more nesting material each year, and old nests may be 5 feet around and 20 feet deep. The birds put aromatic leaves in their nests to control parasites. Chemicals in the leaves act as natural insecticides.

The golden eagle was important to the culture of many Native American tribes. They revered the bird and wore its feathers as part of their ceremonial dress.

NESTING: Pair shares incubation of the 2 white eggs, which hatch in about 6 weeks. Nestlings fledge in 65 to 75 days.

PLUMAGE: Dark brown overall with a light-brown head.

SIZE: Up to 40 inches; males are smaller.

CALL: A sharp, loud "*keeer.*"

HABITAT: Open terrain in mountainous or rugged hilly areas.

NORTHERN HARRIER
Circus cyaneus

Northern harrier; **group:** bird of prey; **family:** hawk.

Northern harriers are interesting hawks that have special plumage and hearing that is similar to owls. This makes them fearsome hunters. Harriers have a round facial disc that gathers sounds and helps them locate prey. They fly low over grasslands and open fields searching the ground with their eyes and ears for small rodents, small rabbits, and other prey.

Though most birds of prey nest in trees or cliffs, northern harrier pairs build a small nest of grasses on level ground hidden among grasses or clover. Harriers will also roost on the ground outside of breeding season. Sometimes you'll even find them roosting with short-eared owls.

Northern harriers have very interesting eyes. Ornithologists believe that hawks see what humans would see if they were using binoculars with eight-power magnification!

NESTING: Female incubates the 5 bluish-white eggs about 31 days. Nestlings fledge in about a month.

PLUMAGE: Both sexes have a white rump patch. Males are mostly silver gray, and females and juveniles are medium brown.

SIZE: 19 inches, and females are larger than males.

CALL: A sharp cry.

HABITAT: Open fields, grasslands, and wetland borders.

RED-TAILED HAWK
Buteo jamaicensis

The red-tailed hawk is the most widespread and abundant North American hawk. It is often seen soaring over open country or perched on fence posts, trees, or power-line poles. This bird of prey feeds on rodents, rabbits, birds, and reptiles. But it has nothing on the world's most dangerous hunters—humans. In the East, the red-tailed hawk population was severely reduced by bounty hunting. Even unintentionally humans inflict damage. Use of DDT (an insecticide) in the 1960s and 1970s damaged hawk populations.

The red-tailed hawk has strong preservation tactics. The female begins incubating the eggs as soon as they are laid. The first egg can hatch several days before any siblings hatch. This is a natural protection. In times of little food, the older nestlings get fed and the younger ones die. This insures that at least some nestlings will live.

NESTING: Clutch of 2 or 3 white or cream (sometimes brown-spotted) eggs hatches in about 32 days. Nestlings fledge in 6 to 7 weeks.

PLUMAGE: Mostly brown with cream-colored breast and brown breast band. But body color can vary from light tan to brown to black. Orange-red tail feathers are distinctive.

SIZE: 20-25 inches, with a wing-span over four feet wide.

CALL: A drawn out *"keeerrrr."*

HABITAT: Open woodlands and grasslands, often mixed with farmland.

Red-tailed hawk; **group:** bird of prey; **family:** hawk.

AMERICAN KESTREL
Falco sparverius

Few birds of prey are as beautiful as North America's smallest falcon, the American kestrel. Unlike other falcons, male and female kestrels can be distinguished by their coloring. A kestrel poised in graceful flight can explode into a head-long dive toward prey on its long, pointed wings. But this common bird of prey is best known for hovering and watching the ground for a possible meal. The American kestrel hunts crickets, grasshoppers, large beetles, small rodents (including mice and voles), small lizards, and even small birds.

American kestrels usually nest in tree cavities, but a mated pair may use nest boxes, or even a bare cliff ledge. Nest boxes and tree cavities are in great demand!

NESTING: Pair incubates the 4 or 5 white eggs about 30 days. Nestlings fledge in about a month.

PLUMAGE: The male has a red-brown back and tail, gray-blue upper wings, and light orange-brown breast. The female has a rusty-brown back, upper wings, and tail; and a cream breast. Both sexes have two distinct vertical stripes on each side of their white faces, gray heads, and black spots on their napes.

SIZE: 10 inches.

CALL: A shrill *"killy-killy-killy."*

HABITAT: Open areas, from grasslands and deserts to woodland borders, agricultural land, and edges of residential areas.

American kestrel; **group:** bird of prey; **family:** falcon.

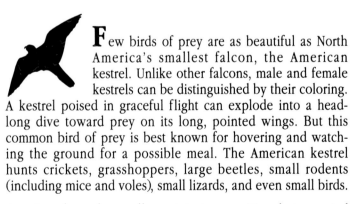

PEREGRINE FALCON
Falco peregrinus

Peregrine falcon; **group:** *bird of prey;* **family:** *falcon.*

With physical features that include a heavy body and broad shoulders, a long tail, and long, pointed wings, perhaps no other bird is so gifted for fast, maneuverable flight than the peregrine falcon. It can reach record-breaking speeds of more than 200 miles per hour during a spectacular dive. The adults perform breathtaking aerial breeding displays prior to egg-laying. Peregrine means "wanderer." They have the most extensive range of any bird.

Peregrine falcons were nearly driven to extinction by pesticides used from the 1940s to the 1970s, but a captive breeding and reintroduction program has re-established many breeding populations. In fact, some birds have been released from city skyscrapers and have successfully adapted to nesting there, where they feed on city pigeons. (Peregrine falcons usually nest on ledges on steep cliffs known as aeries, but a nesting pair may use an old hawk or raven nest.) Peregrine falcons feed mostly on birds.

NESTING: Pair incubates the 3 or 5 white or pinkish (brown-marked) eggs about 30 days. Nestlings fledge in 5 to 6 weeks.

PLUMAGE: Slate gray above, white with variable dark markings below, and a hoodlike black head.

SIZE: 18 inches.

CALL: A sharp, high-pitched cry.

HABITAT: Mountainous areas with open country. Introduced into inner cities.

One of the most common owls in wooded areas of the eastern United States, the eastern screech-owl is often found in residential areas. These little owls are rarely seen, but in the cover of night's darkness they seek out their next meal. They are fierce predators for their size, and they use their specialized eyesight and hearing to locate prey in the dark, and their sharp talons and beak to capture and dispatch that prey. Not only are they expert hunters, they are also diverse hunters. The eastern screech-owl will eat small mammals, insects, gamebirds, earthworms, snakes, snails, even fish and crayfish!

Screech-owls have interesting roommates. They bring live blind snakes to their nest cavities. These snakes stay and live in the debris of the nest and eat insects and larvae. They may reduce insect parasites that attack the owlets. In fact, the owlets from nests with snakes grow faster and have a lower death rate than the owlets from nests without snakes!

NESTING: Pair incubates the 4 or 5 white eggs for 26 days. Owlets fledge in about 4 weeks.

PLUMAGE: Gray or red-brown plumage with black and white mottling.

SIZE: 9 inches.

CALL: A trilling call, sometimes descending in pitch.

HABITAT: Open woodlands.

EASTERN SCREECH-OWL
Otus asio

Eastern screech-owl; **group:** *bird of prey;* **family:** *owl.*

Great horned owls are the most dangerous predators of the night. These owls are large and take prey that varies in size from mice to rabbits to medium-size birds. Owls' eyes are adapted for the night—their eyes can see in very low light. But their real strength is their ears—they can hunt by sound alone. Even their wing feathers are specialized for night hunting—they are soft and fluffy for silent flight.

Great horned owls are named for their two hornlike tufts of feathers that look like ears, but their ears are hidden beneath their feathers. The tufts that look like ears are really not. They can show the owl's mood, they help other owls recognize individual owls, and they make the owl look like a mammal for defense.

Great horned owls nest very early—in the north their eggs may freeze. Sometimes they may be nesting while a late snowstorm rages. The parents cache prey, which usually freezes. The parents incubate the food to thaw it. The original frozen dinner!

GREAT HORNED OWL
Bubo virginianus

Great horned owl; **group:** bird of prey; **family:** owl.

NESTING: Pair incubates the 2 or 4 white eggs about 30 days. Eggs hatch in 2-day intervals. Owlets fledge in about 5 weeks.

PLUMAGE: Gray-brown overall.

SIZE: 20 to 24 inches.

SONG: A deep hooting, "*Who's awake? Me, too.*"

HABITAT: A variety of habitats from moist woodlands to deserts.

BURROWING OWL
Athene cunicularia

Burrowing owl; **group:** bird of prey; **family:** owl.

Why dig a burrow when you can use an abandoned one made by a prairie dog, ground squirrel, badger, or armadillo? This owl does just that. Burrowing owls often return to the same burrow for many years. This bird can be seen as it perches on its long legs on a fence post or on the rim of its burrow. Burrowing owls hunt day and night, usually hovering over prey before pouncing on it from above. They hunt mostly small rodents, but they also hunt lizards, birds, large insects, frogs, and snakes.

Some populations of burrowing owls are declining. In order to control squirrel and prairie dog populations, people often use poison. The problem is that often these owls are poisoned instead of or along with the squirrels and prairie dogs. Also, humans will destroy burrows to get rid of the squirrels and prairie dogs—but again the owls are also injured.

NESTING: Female incubates the 6 to 11 white eggs, which hatch in 21 to 28 days. Nestlings fledge in about 4 weeks.

PLUMAGE: Adults are brown above and lighter brown below, with white spotting overall. Males are slightly darker in color.

SIZE: 9 1/2 inches.

CALL: Rattling "*kek-kek-ke-ke-kek.*"

HABITAT: Open grasslands, prairies, and savannas. Sometimes found near airports, golf courses, and open areas near residential developments.

The ring-necked pheasant is possibly the best-known gamebird in the world. Native to east-central Asia, this bird has been introduced into Europe and North America and now lives in most temperate areas of the Northern Hemisphere. The first person to try to introduce this bird to the United States was the son-in-law of Benjamin Franklin, Richard Bache. He was unsuccessful, but Judge O. N. Denny, the U.S. consul general in Shanghai, China, introduced the bird to Oregon in 1801.

The ring-necked pheasant expanded its range naturally, and with the help of other introductions. It now lives throughout most areas of the United States, as well as southern Canada. Its beautiful coloration, wary behavior, swift flight, ability to run quickly through cover, and high reproduction rate have endeared it to birders and sport hunters alike. Ring-necked pheasants feed on insects and seeds, including waste grain.

NESTING: Female incubates the 10 to 12 eggs about 24 days. Nestlings fledge in about 12 days.

PLUMAGE: The male has an iridescent-green head; white neck ring; rich brown, orange, and golden body; a black-banded long brown tail; and bare red facial patches. Females are tan, mottled with black and brown.

SIZE: 33 inches.

SONG: Male crows, similar to a rooster.

HABITAT: Agricultural areas bordered by brushy areas, grasslands, open woodland edges, and wetlands.

RING-NECKED PHEASANT
Phasianus colchicus

Ring-necked pheasant; **group:** *gamebird;* **family:** *pheasant.*

If woodland birds could form a band, the ruffed grouse would be the drummer. Males drum by cupping their wings and beating them rapidly against the air, usually while standing on a log. After drumming, the male spreads its tail, crest, and neck ruff feathers. The male ruffed grouse drums to let other males know that this is his territory and to attract females. A male will mate with more than one female.

Ruffed grouse feed on buds, leaves, seeds, berries, tree flowers, and insects. Even though an adult grouse eats mostly vegetation (up to 80 percent), young grouse need more protein to grow. They eat insects and small animals that are high in protein. The female not only makes sure her chicks get fed well, she also is their protector. Should a predator threaten, she will lure it away or even perform a distraction display so the chicks can get to safety.

NESTING: Clutch of 8 to 12 buff eggs hatches in about 24 days. Chicks can fly short distances in about 10 days.

PLUMAGE: Both brown and gray color phases have lighter belly and black and white spotting, with black tail band.

SIZE: 17 inches.

CALL: Cackling calls.

HABITAT: Northern mixed deciduous and pine woodlands with undergrowth. Aspen forests are preferred.

RUFFED GROUSE
Bonasa umbellus

Ruffed grouse; **group:** *gamebird;* **family:** *pheasant.*

SAGE GROUSE
Centrocercus urophasianus

Sage grouse; **group:** *gamebird;*
family: *pheasant.*

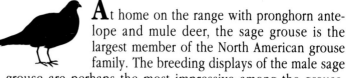

At home on the range with pronghorn antelope and mule deer, the sage grouse is the largest member of the North American grouse family. The breeding displays of the male sage grouse are perhaps the most impressive among the grouse. The big males spread their long, pointed tail feathers into a fan that they hold erect while partly spreading their wings at their sides. Their heads are held high and they inflate the large air sacs in their necks until they hang almost to the ground. They display toward males in adjoining territories on the display ground (lek). Some of the dances of Native American tribes are imitations of the circling foot-stomping displays.

When the smaller females visit the lek to mate, the males erupt into a flurry of displays. This is accompanied by popping noises made when the males discharge air from their air sacs. The females mate with the most dominant males, which means that the best genes are used to reproduce.

NESTING: Female incubates the 6 to 9 tan or olive (brown-spotted) eggs about 25 days. Nestlings fledge in 7 to 10 days.

PLUMAGE: Both sexes are cryptic brown, white, and black, with a dark-brown belly and long tail feathers. Males have a black throat and upper breast, and a white breast.

SIZE: 28 inches.

CALL: Repetitive clucking.

HABITAT: Western sagebrush plains and foothills.

SHARP-TAILED GROUSE
Tympanuchus phasianellus

Sharp-tailed grouse; **group:**
gamebird; **family:** *pheasant.*

Haunting, eerie calls fill the crisp, early spring morning air over the prairie grasslands, accompanied by an occasional cackle. In the trampled grassland arena, about 15 male sharp-tailed grouse have partitioned off pieces of turf where they periodically break into a frenzied dance. With their wings spread, head and neck outstretched, and tail erect they stamp their feet against the frozen ground as they inflate the purple air sacs in their necks and call—exactly like generations of grouse before them. Their inflatable air sacs act as resonating chambers for this loud "booming" call. The behavior is escalated when a female visits the lek and makes her way to the center of the dancing grounds to choose a mate.

Though sharp-tailed grouse are the best fliers in the grouse family, they would rather stay on the ground, like other grouse. But it is such a strong flyer that it can escape from hawks and owls in the air!

NESTING: Female incubates the 10 to 14 tan (brown-spotted) eggs for 21 to 24 days. Nestlings fledge after a week.

PLUMAGE: Well-camouflaged plumage with mottled white, tan, brown, and black.

SIZE: 17 inches.

CALL: A sharp, repeated cackling.

HABITAT: Open grasslands, sagebrush, and other bushy cover, and agricultural areas.

WILD TURKEY
Meleagris gallopavo

Wild turkey; **group:** *gamebird;* **family:** *pheasant.*

The wild turkey is one of the best known American birds. Even small children can imitate its *"gobble, gobble"* call. Surely, no Thanksgiving Day passes without mention of the wild turkey. The domestic form of the turkey has spawned a large world-wide poultry industry. Turkeys feed on insects, seeds, acorns, berries, plant buds, and leaves.

During their mating displays, male wild turkeys (toms) spread out their large tails in a semicircular fan, hold their wings down at their sides, and show off their bright red and blue neck skins. The males gobble occasionally all year long, but the sound fills the spring woods when breeding season comes. Each tom has his own small clearing, where he tries to lure females in to breed. He struts from side to side to entice the females. The tom mates with as many females as he can.

Wildlife biologists reintroduced wild turkeys into many parts of the country where they had disappeared. Today, more wild turkeys roam the forests!

NESTING: Hen incubates the 10 to 12 eggs for 4 weeks. Chicks fledge after 1 week.

PLUMAGE: Mostly brown with some iridescent coloration. They have bare heads and necks.

SIZE: Males are larger than females and may measure 46 inches in length.

SONG: *"Gobble, gobble, gobble."*

HABITAT: Open woodlands and bordering agricultural areas.

Few birds offer as startling an introduction to birders as northern bobwhites. Flocks of these small quail erupt into the air if you startle them where they hide in bushes. One after another they whir up and away on quick wingbeats, no less startled than the people they catch off guard. Northern bob-whites feed on insects, seeds, leaves, buds, berries, fruit, and agricultural grains.

During breeding season, male bobwhites are aggressive. But when breeding season is over, both males and females form coveys of 25 to 30 birds. If they spot danger, the covey of birds will stand still. If startled, they erupt into the air. At night, the covey forms a circle with all the birds facing outward. This not only provides warmth on a cold winter night, it also gives each bird an unobscured path in which to get away should danger approach. And danger cannot approach without some bird facing it and warning the other birds!

NESTING: Pair incubates the 6 to 18 eggs about 24 days. Chicks fledge in about 6 days.

PLUMAGE: Mottled brown above and brown and white below. The throat patch and eye stripes that extend from the bill to the nape are white in males and tan in females.

SIZE: 10 inches.

SONG: Whistled *"bob-white."*

HABITAT: Brushy fields and grassy, open woodlands; agricultural fields.

NORTHERN BOBWHITE
Colinus virginianus

Northern bobwhite; **group:** *gamebird;* **family:** *pheasant.*

CALIFORNIA QUAIL
Callipepla californica

*California quail; **group:** gamebird; **family:** pheasant.*

If you're hiking along the scrub- and cha-parral-covered foothills in the western United States, watch out. Though not dangerous, a covey of California quail erupting from bushes is quite startling. The California quail is beau-tiful, and both males and females have large black topknot feathers. Quail are landbirds that find food on the ground or in bushes. They rarely take to the air except to escape danger, but even then they may first try running away. These quail feed on green plants, acorns, fruit, berries, and some insects.

California quail have a natural form of birth control. In dry years, the quail do not breed. Subterranean-clover, one of the quail's main foods, has a higher content of phytoestrogens when it is dry. This is a hormone that prevents the birds from reproducing. When rains are ample, the birds reproduce nor-mally. Nature takes care of these birds.

NESTING: Female incubates the 12 to 16 white eggs for 18 to 23 days. Chicks fledge in about 10 days.

PLUMAGE: Brown wings; gray breast, back, and tail; and white-scaled belly. The male has a black throat bordered by white and a black plume on its crown. The female has a gray-brown, white-scaled head, with a smaller plume.

SIZE: 10 inches.

CALL: A cackling, three-note call.

HABITAT: Brushy foothills, open woodlands, overgrown canyons, and river valleys.

KILLDEER
Charadrius vociferus

The killdeer is the best actor in the bird world. Although many other birds perform distraction displays, this common shorebird has its act down pat. When an intruder comes too near the bird's nest or its chicks, the adult will sneak away for a distance, then attract attention to itself with its piercing, incessant call. The killdeer then begins its act. It spreads its tail and droops one wing to the side as though it were bro-ken. Its walk becomes wobbly and it appears to be easy prey. Should the predator get too close, the killdeer takes to the air, its wing healed. But it may land and resume its theatrics, even alternating wings, if the intruder doesn't leave!

In hot areas, parents will soak their belly feathers with water to cool off the eggs. Killdeer chicks begin peeping inside their eggs a few days before hatching. They begin to feed them-selves a few hours after hatching.

NESTING: Pair incubates the tan (brown-marked) eggs for 24 to 28 days. Chicks fledge in about 25 days.

PLUMAGE: Plumage is brown above and white below, with black and white bands on their breast and head.

SIZE: 10 inches.

CALL: A loud, piercing, repeated "*teee-teee*" or "*kill-deer.*"

HABITAT: Wetland shorelines, open areas with short vegetation, agricultural fields, athletic fields, even lawns.

*Killdeer; **group:** shorebird, gulls, and terns; **family:** plover.*

AMERICAN OYSTERCATCHER
Haematopus palliatus

The American oystercatcher's name is rather misleading. It is not hard to catch oysters and other mollusks, after all, they are not fast-moving prey like insects and fish! But it is difficult to get the meat inside. The oystercatcher has a bright red, long, stout, angular bill that is perfectly designed for breaking into this hard-shelled food. Prying apart clams is difficult, yet oystercatchers do it easily—usually less than 30 seconds! Young birds learn one of two ways to open the shells. A "stabber" sneaks up and plunges its bill between the shells before the oyster can snap shut. A "hammerer" shatters one shell with a rapid series of blows and then inserts its bill into the hole.

This boldly colored black and white shorebird lives along rocky or sandy ocean shorelines and islands, where it probes for and searches out mollusks and other invertebrates that live in the ocean, including crabs and worms. It may be seen along the Atlantic and Gulf Coasts and the Pacific in southern California.

American oystercatcher; **group:** *shorebird, gulls, and terns;* **family:** *oystercatcher.*

NESTING: Pair incubates the 3 cream or olive (brown-marked) eggs for 24 to 29 days. Young become independent at about 5 weeks.

PLUMAGE: White belly, wing patch, and rump; black head, neck, and tail; and dark-brown back and wings.

SIZE: 18 inches.

CALL: A shrill *"kleep."*

HABITAT: Sandy or rocky ocean shorelines or mud flats.

BLACK-NECKED STILT

Himantopus mexicanus

Black-necked stilt; **group:** *shorebird, gulls, and terns;* **family:** *avocet and stilt.*

When a predator enters the nesting area of a pair of black-necked stilts, the birds become masters at leading the predator away from the eggs or young. First the birds fly overhead calling loudly and diving at the intruder; in a nesting colony several pairs will join in a loud and wild flurry of activity. If unsuccessful with this tactic, one of the birds may pretend to be injured by crouching and dragging one wing at its side to divert the predator's attention away from the nests or young. Black-necked stilts live in shallow-water wetlands where they wade to search for food, which includes small shrimp and other small invertebrates, including brine flies.

The black-necked stilt has a way to keep itself and its nest air-conditioned on hot days. It keeps its ventral feathers wet by making many trips to the water. This not only keeps the bird cool, but it also keeps the eggs or nestlings from becoming too hot in the sun. It can make up to 100 trips a day!

NESTING: Pair incubates the 4 tan (brown-marked) eggs for 22 to 26 days. Chicks fledge in about a month.

PLUMAGE: Black above and white below, with pink legs and feet.

SIZE: 14 inches.

CALL: *"Kek-kek, kek-kek."*

HABITAT: Shallow wetlands.

AMERICAN AVOCET

Recurvirostra americana

American avocet; **group:** shorebird, gulls, and terns; **family:** avocet and stilt.

Considered the most beautiful shorebird, the American avocet is among the most graceful of all American birds. Avocets have partly webbed feet and, although they usually wade in shallow water, they do occasionally swim. It is the only shorebird with a curved, upturned bill. It sweeps its bill back and forth beneath the water, finding food by feel. It also uses its bill to probe for food in the mud. Avocets feed mostly on crustaceans and aquatic insects and some aquatic vegetation and seeds.

To attract a mate, the male American avocet performs a balletlike courtship display with bowing, open-wing prancing, and sweeping its bill back and forth. American avocet pairs nest in loose colonies or alone. And when a predator tries to enter a colony of avocets, it is in for a surprise. The colony will mob the predator to drive it away. The colony can also perform a group distraction display to divert the predator.

NESTING: Pair builds nest of dried plants and feathers on sand or gravel. Usual clutch of 4 olive-buff (brown- or black-marked) eggs hatches in 22 to 29 days. Chicks fledge in 4 to 5 weeks.

PLUMAGE: White belly, breast, and back; mostly black wings with some white. Head and neck feathers of breeding adults are rust, but molt to a gray-white during nonbreeding season. Legs and feet are bright blue.

SIZE: 18 inches.

CALL: A loud *"weet-weet."*

HABITAT: Shallow freshwater, alkaline, and brackish wetlands.

SPOTTED SANDPIPER

Actitis macularia

The spotted sandpiper is a small, common, solitary shorebird that has one of the most unusual mating strategies of any North American bird. Female spotted sandpipers may lay up to five complete clutches of eggs in nests built by male mates, although two or three clutches are most common. The males incubate the eggs and raise the brood of chicks. Since a clutch can be four eggs, a single female could produce 20 fledglings in one nesting season! Experienced females have more mates and produce more eggs, chicks, and fledglings. This breeding system (one female mates with many males) is called polyandry, and it is very rare among birds.

Spotted sandpipers feed on small aquatic invertebrates, including insects and worms. It is easy to recognize spotted sandpipers by their behavior. They are constantly bobbing and teetering—they are quite amusing to watch!

Spotted sandpiper; **group:** shorebird, gulls, and terns; **family:** sandpiper and phalarope.

NESTING: Male builds nest and incubates the clutch of 4 greenish or buff eggs, which hatches in 20 to 24 days. Nestlings fledge in 17 to 21 days.

PLUMAGE: Both sexes have medium-brown plumage above and white with brown spots below.

SIZE: 7 inches.

CALL: A shrill *"peet-weet."*

HABITAT: Shallow wetlands or shorelines.

AMERICAN WOODCOCK
Scolopax minor

*American woodcock; **group:** shorebird, gulls, and terns; **family:** sandpiper and phalarope.*

The spectacular flight display of the male American woodcock is one of spring's most exciting attractions. Most aerial displays are done at night, when only the telltale whistling of their wings lets humans know what is happening. This loud whistling is made when the bird vibrates its wings. However, patient observers can see these courtship display flights at dawn and dusk. Woodcocks are usually awake at night, and so are rarely seen except when flushed from the forest floor.

The American woodcock mainly eats earthworms, but it will also eat insects. An American woodcock has an unusual method of finding earthworms. It pounds its feet on moist earth, maybe to set the earthworms moving. Then it sticks its bill, which has many sensitive nerve endings, in up to its nostrils to find the earthworms. And even more amazing, this bird eats more than its weight in earthworms each day. That's a lot of worms!

NESTING: Female performs all nesting, incubating, and raising of young. Clutch of 4 light-cinnamon eggs hatches in about 20 days. Chicks fledge in about 2 weeks.

PLUMAGE: Mostly tan with a black nape.

SIZE: 11 inches.

SONG: "*Peent.*"

HABITAT: Moist woodlands, thickets along boggy streams, and mixed forests.

WILSON'S PHALAROPE
Phalaropus tricolor

*Wilson's phalarope; **group:** shorebird, gulls, and terns; **family:** sandpiper and phalarope.*

Wilson's phalaropes have one of the most unusual breeding strategies in the bird world—the roles of the sexes are reversed! The female Wilson's phalarope is the most colorful of the sexes and she courts the male. Each female mates with a number of males. Each male builds a nest for the female to lay a clutch of four eggs in, after which the male incubates the eggs and raises the chicks. Occasionally a female may court another male and lay another clutch in his nest. Males make several scrapes on the ground. The female chooses one to lay her eggs in.

Wilson's phalaropes feed on small aquatic invertebrates and seeds of aquatic plants. Their most interesting method of feeding is to whirl in circles to stir food items off the wetland bottom.

NESTING: Male incubates the 4 buff eggs, which hatch in 16 to 21 days. Fledging time unknown.

PLUMAGE: Females more colorful with a gray breast, back, and nape; a black line through the eyes extending along both sides of the neck where it is bordered by rusty red; wings are slate gray at tips and rust red near shoulders. Males have less distinct coloring.

SIZE: 9 inches.

CALL: Hoarse "*work.*"

HABITAT: Shallow freshwater and saline wetlands.

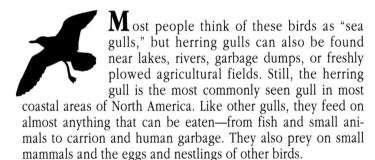

The unceasing noise and activity at a ring-billed gull nesting colony can be too much for some people. Hundreds of adult birds fly overhead bringing food into the colony to feed growing chicks, while others fly off to collect more food—fish, insects, aquatic invertebrates, and the young of small birds and mammals. The adults may be loud, but the growing chicks are also vocal when they beg for food.

Ring-billed gulls have increased their numbers. They are one of the few birds that has benefited by the development of humans. They are now found far inland. They follow farmers plowing their fields to get insects thrown into the air by the plows. And a favorite site is the local landfill!

Ring-billed gulls nest in large colonies on small islands in inland lakes where nests may be only a few feet apart. They may share the nesting island with other colonial-nesting birds.

NESTING: Pair builds nest and incubates the 2 to 4 white (brown-marked) eggs about 3 weeks. Chicks fledge in 3 weeks.

PLUMAGE: White head, breast, belly, upper back, and tail; light-gray back; and black-tipped wings. It has yellow legs, feet, and bill with a distinctive black line across the end.

SIZE: 17 inches.

CALL: A loud cry or laughlike call.

HABITAT: Inland lakes, rivers, coastal areas, and garbage dumps.

RING-BILLED GULL
Larus delawarensis

Ring-billed gull; **group:** *shorebird, gulls, and terns;* **family:** *gull and tern.*

HERRING GULL
Larus argentatus

Most people think of these birds as "sea gulls," but herring gulls can also be found near lakes, rivers, garbage dumps, or freshly plowed agricultural fields. Still, the herring gull is the most commonly seen gull in most coastal areas of North America. Like other gulls, they feed on almost anything that can be eaten—from fish and small animals to carrion and human garbage. They also prey on small mammals and the eggs and nestlings of other birds.

Herring gulls nest in large breeding colonies on beaches, or islands in fresh or salt water. The pair builds the nest with grass, lichens, or other available plants. The fledglings in a herring gull colony are kept in groups called creches—similar to day-care centers. Supervision of the young is left to a few guardians so that both parents can bring food back to their young.

NESTING: Pair builds nest and incubates the 3 eggs for 24 to 28 days. Nestlings fledge in about 5 weeks.

PLUMAGE: Adults are white with a light-gray back and wings, and black wing tips. They have pink webbed feet and a yellow bill. Immature birds are mostly brown, and molt three times before they attain their adult plumage in their fourth year.

SIZE: 25 inches.

CALL: A loud cry or multisyllabic, laughlike call.

HABITAT: Lakes, rivers, and ocean coasts.

Herring gull; **group:** *shorebird, gulls, and terns;* **family:** *gull and tern.*

COMMON TERN
Sterna hirundo

Common tern; **group:** *shorebird, gulls, and terns;* **family:** *gull and tern.*

The streamlined common tern spreads its forked tail wide and hovers over the water for a moment, then dives headfirst into the water. It rises quickly out of the water with a minnow in its bill and flies off to its nest. Terns are closely related to gulls, and they share similar habitats. But terns are smaller; have pointed wings; smaller, more pointed bills; and they plunge headfirst into water after fish.

In the late 1800s, common terns were nearly hunted to extinction for their feathers. The fashion of the day included women's hats decorated with bird feathers, even entire wings. In 1903, plumes sold for $32 per ounce—twice the price of gold! In 1886, ornithologist Frank Chapman conducted a bird survey along the streets of Manhattan. Birds adorned three quarters of the 700 women's hats he saw—he counted nearly 40 species of birds. Unfortunately, one of the most common was the common tern. Thank goodness that fashions change and that people have begun to value birds for more than just decoration!

NESTING: Pair incubates the 3 tan (brown-marked) eggs for 21 to 27 days. Chicks fledge in less than 4 weeks.

PLUMAGE: Gray above, white below, with a black crown and nape. Red-orange legs, feet, and bill.

SIZE: 14 inches.

CALL: A high-pitched *"keerr."*

HABITAT: Wetland shorelines.

BLACK SKIMMER
Rynchops niger

The black skimmer is a unique bird. It is the only North American bird that has a longer lower bill than upper bill. It also has a unique way to fish, which is why its lower bill is longer. This bird glides above the water with its lower bill cutting through the water's surface. When its lower bill hits a fish, the upper bill snaps shut. Because the friction of the water wears down the lower bill, it grows faster than the upper bill. Black skimmers feed mostly on small fish, although they may also capture small crustaceans.

Black skimmers nest on sandbars or sandy island beaches in loose colonies, sometimes with terns or gulls. The lower bills of young skimmers do not grow longer than the upper bills until they mature.

Black skimmers have one amazing trick that is necessary for a bird that looks at the water much of the day. They can narrow their pupils to thin vertical slits to cut glare on a sunny day. So who needs sunglasses?

NESTING: Pair incubates the 4 whitish eggs about 3 weeks. Nestlings fledge in about 24 days.

PLUMAGE: Black above and white below, with a black-tipped red bill and red legs and feet. In winter, they have a white collar.

SIZE: 18 inches.

HABITAT: Ocean coasts and coastal wetlands.

Black skimmer; **group:** *shorebird, gulls, and terns;* **family:** *skimmer.*

One of the most common city-dwelling birds, rock doves are often called pigeons. The original wild stock came from the Middle East, but were introduced and spread throughout most areas of the world. They may have been the first bird ever domesticated. Rock doves are social and are usually found in flocks. They feed on seeds and grains and a variety of human refuse, and will visit backyard feeders. Rock doves become very tame and you often see people feeding them in city parks.

Rock doves have an amazing ability to return to their homes—called homing ability. They are fast and able to travel long distances. They were used for centuries as carriers of messages long before telegraphs or telephones. In fact, that was one of the reasons they were introduced to North America. Another reason they were brought here was to be used for food.

NESTING: Pair incubates the 2 white eggs for 16 to 19 days. Nestlings fledge in 25 or 26 days.

PLUMAGE: Variations of gray, brown, black, or white; all have a white rump.

SIZE: 14 inches.

CALL: A cooing call.

HABITAT: Near people, cities, towns, and farmyards.

ROCK DOVE
Columba livia

Rock dove; group: landbird; family: pigeon and dove.

MOURNING DOVE

Zenaida macroura

Mourning dove; group: landbird; family: pigeon and dove.

The mourning dove is the most widespread and common North American dove. Its mournful, cooing call is a favorite. Unfortunately for the mourning dove, it is also a favorite among hunters. It is the most widely hunted and harvested gamebird. Mourning doves feed on waste grains and seeds.

Mourning doves are among the first birds to begin the nesting season in many regions. The graceful male glides and circles over its nesting territory. When a dove is incubating its eggs in the hot desert, it will pant, much like a dog pants. This releases heat from its body, which lowers the temperature of the eggs to about 95°F—even if the daytime temperature is 115°F. To feed its young, a mourning dove produces pigeon milk. This is not really milk, but a protein that is rich in fat. Pigeon milk is produced by the lining of the bird's crop.

NESTING: Clutch of 2 to 3 white eggs hatches in about 14 days. Nestlings fledge in about 2 weeks.

PLUMAGE: Male and female are mostly light brown with some iridescent violet, pink, and green feathers in the neck, which are prominent during breeding season.

SIZE: 12 inches.

SONG: A mournful *"coo, coo."* Their wings also make a whistling sound when they fly.

HABITAT: Everywhere except dense forests and wetlands.

Best known as a cartoon character that is chased by the coyote, the roadrunner is actually a bird that lives in the southwest—from Texas to California. The greater roadrunner is a bird that lives on the ground; it usually flies only to escape danger. In fact, roadrunners can run at speeds up to 15 miles per hour, and they are extremely agile. Folklore holds that roadrunners are so quick that they can corral rattlesnakes with cactus spines. This is not true, but they are quick enough to avoid cars. Roadrunners are seldom seen dead along roadsides.

Greater roadrunners are efficient predators that eat insects, lizards, snakes, birds, and small mammals. Roadrunners run or walk in a strutting fashion with their crested heads and long tails held upright. They raise and lower their crest and tail when curious or alarmed. It is no wonder that Mexicans call this bird *paisano,* which means "countryman."

NESTING: Pair incubates the 4 to 6 white eggs about 3 weeks. Nestlings fledge in about 18 days.

PLUMAGE: Mostly olive brown with white markings, a white throat and belly, long tail feathers, and a dark-brown crest.

SIZE: 23 inches.

SONG: Descending dovelike *"cooing."*

HABITAT: Arid scrub or chaparral. Sometimes seen in agricultural areas and residential parks or golf courses.

GREATER ROADRUNNER
Geococcyx californianus

Greater roadrunner; **group:** *landbird;* **family:** *cuckoo.*

Hummingbirds are the only birds that can fly backward, forward, up, down, sideways, upside down, and hover. The ruby-throated hummingbird is a unique bird found in the eastern United States and southern Canada, where it is the only breeding hummingbird. Ruby-throated hummingbirds beat their wings over 70 times per second while flying forward—their wings are a blur of motion to human eyes.

Ruby-throated hummingbirds feed mostly on flower nectar. They supplement their diet with insects and spiders. Hummingbirds have such a fast metabolism that they must eat nearly all day long. When they return north from their wintering grounds, their flower sources may not have begun to bloom. But they survive because they are very adaptable eaters. They can eat only insects and spiders if they have to.

NESTING: Female incubates clutch of 2 tiny white eggs, which hatches in 11 to 13 days. Nestlings fledge within 3 weeks.

PLUMAGE: Males are green above, green and white below, with an iridescent-red throat.

Females are green above, white below, with white throats.

SIZE: 4 inches.

CALL: *"Tew."*

HABITAT: Open areas with flowering plants, including residential areas and suburban parks.

RUBY-THROATED HUMMINGBIRD
Archilochus colubris

Ruby-throated hummingbird;
group: *landbird;* **family:**
hummingbird.

BLACK-CHINNED HUMMINGBIRD

Archilochus alexandri

Black-chinned hummingbird; **group:** landbird; **family:** hummingbird.

Hummingbirds are winged marvels that speed between flowers and nest. Their wings blur in superfast motion. The black-chinned hummingbird is the most widespread western hummingbird. Black-chinned hummers feed on flower nectar and very small insects and spiders.

The male does a spectacular aerial "swinging pendulum" courtship display. The male will fly along a shallow U; at the top of each side he makes a sound by flapping his wings. At the bottom of the U, he makes a high-pitched, long note. Once a pair breeds, the female does all nesting work. And the female hummer is a master builder. She builds a small cuplike nest of plant down and spider webs on a tree or shrub limb hidden by leaves. She twirls around inside the nest, pressing her breast into the sides of the nest to mold it to the proper shape. And her nest grows! The 1½-inch nest is able to stretch when the nestlings begin growing.

NESTING: Female incubates the 2 white eggs, which hatch in about 15 days. Nestlings fledge in about 3 weeks.

PLUMAGE: Metallic-green body and white belly. Male has a black throat with a violet border.

SIZE: 3¾ inches.

CALL: *"Chew"* and squeaky chatter.

HABITAT: Lowlands, near waterways and residential areas with flowers and feeders.

BELTED KINGFISHER

Ceryle alcyon

Belted kingfisher; **group:** landbird; **family:** kingfisher.

Watching the belted kingfisher's spectacular headfirst dive into water after a fish is exciting for a new birdwatcher—and even longtime birdwatchers still find it thrilling. The dive may begin from a perch over a pond or from hovering flight. As its name implies, the belted kingfisher catches and feeds mostly on small fish. This bird also eats crayfish and other small aquatic invertebrates and frogs.

Belted kingfishers are usually solitary birds—they only work together as a breeding pair. Though ornithologists think that both parents take care of the young and that the young fledge in 23 days or more, they are not sure. Birdwatchers could learn more about kingfishers by carefully watching the birds' nests and behavior. This is one hobby where amateurs can make big contributions to the body of scientific knowledge. After the young have fledged, the parents teach them how to fish by dropping dead and wounded minnows into the water.

NESTING: Pair builds nest in steep riverbank. Clutch of 6 to 7 white eggs hatches in 24 days. Young fledge in about 23 days.

PLUMAGE: Mostly light blue with a white throat and breast. The blue breast band and broad crest are distinctive. Females have a reddish belly band.

SIZE: 13 inches.

CALL: A long, rattling call.

HABITAT: Rivers and wetlands.

If you live or travel east of the Rocky Mountains, your favorite bird could turn out to be the red-headed woodpecker. You can spot it by its red head, neck, and throat, which show brightly against its black back and white underparts. This woodpecker eats insects it finds on tree trunks and branches. It has a special beak to drill and pry into bark and wood to find food. It can catch insects in flight, and it also eats berries, seeds, and even bird eggs and nestlings!

A nesting pair of red-headed woodpeckers chisels a hole in a dead tree, or a dead branch of a live tree, with their bills. They use this cavity for their nest. Because they have lost much of their nesting habitat to humans, the red-headed woodpecker population is decreasing. This bird competes with starlings, other small woodpeckers, and kestrels for nest cavities. The other birds can be more aggressive than the red-headed woodpecker.

RED-HEADED WOODPECKER
Melanerpes erythrocephalus

Red-headed woodpecker; **group:** *landbird;* **family:** *woodpecker.*

NESTING: Pair incubates the 4 or 5 white eggs, which hatch in 12 to 13 days. Nestlings fledge in about 4 weeks.

PLUMAGE: Both sexes have a bright-red head; white secondary wing feathers, rump, and belly; black back, wing, and tail feath-ers. Juveniles have brown heads and backs.

SIZE: 9 inches.

CALL: A loud *"kweerk."*

HABITAT: Open deciduous woodlands and parks.

DOWNY WOODPECKER
Picoides pubescens

Downy woodpecker; **group:** *landbird;* **family:** *woodpecker.*

This miniature woodpecker creeps along tree trunks and branches searching for food; poking and prodding the bark for insects. It eats seeds, berries, and insects that live in trees. Downy woodpeckers are often found in suburban areas and they visit backyard feeders to eat seeds or suet.

A breeding pair makes a new nesting cavity each year in a dead tree trunk or branch. Some birds try to eat the eggs or nestlings of cavity-nesting birds, so downy woodpeckers often camouflage the entrance of their nest cavity by surrounding it with fungi, lichen, or moss. In the southern part of its range, breeding pairs may have two broods in a season.

Downy woodpeckers do not migrate, and each bird makes a roosting cavity for itself for the winter. They will occasionally use bird boxes for roosting but not for nesting. This woodpecker resembles the hairy woodpecker, but it is smaller.

NESTING: Pair incubates the 4 to 5 white eggs for 12 days. Nestlings fledge in about 3 weeks.

PLUMAGE: Black with white markings and spots above, and white below. Males have a red spot on the nape.

SIZE: 7 inches.

CALL: *"Pick."*

HABITAT: Woodlands, orchards, and suburban areas.

A loud, wild call resounds through the woods, followed by a loud repetitious tapping. Behind all that noise is one of the most common woodpeckers. Northern flickers are easy to identify by their call and their distinctive undulating flight. They hammer on the wood of dead trees to advertise their territories. They will often visit backyard feeders. Flickers prefer ants, but feed on a variety of insects, insect larvae, and eggs. They sometimes feed on seeds and nuts. A flicker's tongue extends three inches beyond its beak, so it is ideally suited to catching ants. Because of its diet, it spends more time on the ground than other woodpeckers.

These industrious woodpeckers excavate nesting cavities in dead wood, and provide nesting sites for a variety of cavity-nesting birds. Northern populations migrate to the United States and Mexico in winter. Three races are recognized: the yellow-shafted (eastern North America), red-shafted (western range), and gilded (desert Southwest).

NORTHERN FLICKER
Colaptes auratus

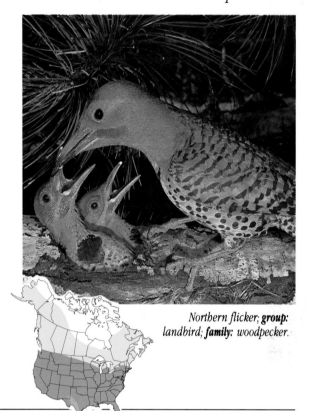

Northern flicker; group: landbird; family: woodpecker.

NESTING: Pair incubates the 5 to 8 white eggs for 11 to 14 days. Nestlings fledge in 25 to 28 days.

PLUMAGE: Gray head with tan cheeks, red nape, brown-barred back and wings, black breast, tan-spotted belly, white rump, and black tail. Males have a black or red "moustache stripe."

SIZE: 12 inches.

CALL: "*Wik-a-wik-a-wik-a-wik.*"

HABITAT: Open woodlands, arid brushlands, and suburban areas.

PILEATED WOODPECKER
Dryocopus pileatus

Pileated woodpecker; group: landbird; family: woodpecker.

A loud *wuka-wuk-a-wuk-a-wuka* call breaks the stillness of the forest, revealing the location of a large, spectacular black-and-white bird that has a distinctive red crest. The pileated woodpecker is the largest of the 21 woodpeckers found in the United States and Canada. It is about the size of a crow! As this impressive woodpecker begins tapping at the trunk of a tree, its sturdy beak breaks away pieces of bark as it chisels a large, oval nesting hole. This regal forest woodpecker prefers mature forests, but has adapted to some lumbered areas, suburban parks, and younger forests. Pileated woodpeckers feed on insects, especially carpenter ants, along with some fruits and nuts.

Adults keep a year-round territory in a mature forest. They maintain their pair bond throughout the winter.

NESTING: Pair excavates nesting cavity and incubates the 4 white eggs for 15 to 18 days. Nestlings fledge in about 4 weeks.

PLUMAGE: Black overall with white face and neck stripes and a distinctive red crest. Males have a red "moustache stripe."

SIZE: 16 inches.

CALL: A loud "*wuka-wuk-a-wuk-a-wuka.*"

HABITAT: Prefers mature woodlands, but may be seen in some lumbered or suburban areas.

Although its name implies that the great crested flycatcher is a large, impressive bird, it is actually small. It measures less than nine inches long. However, this bird's ability to capture flying insects in quick, sometimes hovering flight is great indeed. The great crested flycatcher is as impressive in its pursuit of insects as a falcon diving upon a flock of shorebirds. This flycatcher usually perches on an exposed perch and watches for insects, which the flycatcher then chases until the insects get snapped up in the bird's bill. This bird prefers to feed in the tops of trees. Before some forests were thinned and others were cut down by humans, these birds probably lived in deep forests.

Great crested flycatchers use old woodpecker holes, natural cavities, or birdhouses to build their nests. Their nests often contain snakeskins. Ornithologists don't know why—maybe the snakeskins scare would-be predators.

NESTING: Female incubates the 5 white (brown-, olive-, or lavender-marked) eggs about 2 weeks. Nestlings fledge in 2 to 3 weeks.

PLUMAGE: Dark olive above, gray throat and breast, yellow belly, rust tail, and a thick crest.

SIZE: 9 inches.

CALL: "*Wheep.*"

HABITAT: Open woodlands and orchards.

GREAT CRESTED FLYCATCHER
Myiarchus crinitus

Great crested flycatcher; **group:** perching bird; **family:** tyrant flycatcher.

PURPLE MARTIN
Progne subis

Purple martin; **group:** perching bird; **family:** swallow.

Their name is deceiving—purple martins are actually black swallows. But whatever they are, these birds are favorites among bird lovers. Many people build elaborate houses—martin condominiums—to attract them to their neighborhoods during the summer breeding season. Purple martins are great birds to have around. Not only are they lovely, but they also eat small flying insects, which the birds can catch and eat on the wing. They also drink and even bathe on the wing! But contrary to popular belief, purple martins are not great mosquito catchers. They catch mosquitoes at the same rate as you would if you were riding a bicycle with your mouth open.

Purple martins are cavity nesters. Today most martins probably use artificial cavities placed high on poles, especially in the eastern part of their range. Even many years ago, Native Americans were attracting purple martins by placing hollowed gourds near their lodgings.

NESTING: Female incubates the 4 or 5 white eggs, which hatch in 15 to 18 days. Nestlings fledge in about 4 weeks.

PLUMAGE: Males are a dark, iridescent blue. Females are similar above, and gray below. Both have a forked tail.

SIZE: 8 inches.

CALL: Short chirping notes.

HABITAT: Open and rural areas, especially near water.

BARN SWALLOW
Hirundo rustica

Barn swallow; **group:** perching bird; **family:** swallow.

Few birds rival a barn swallow's flying ability. This bird seems to fly with enthusiasm and glee, and lots of energy, as it makes quick turns and dips while it pursues small flying insects. Barn swallows are social birds that are usually seen in loose flocks. They nest in small colonies made up of several nesting pairs. Barn swallows eat flying insects and spend more time in the air than almost any other landbird.

Both male and female barn swallows share nest-building, incubation, feeding, and brooding of the nestlings. These birds often return to the same colony to nest year after year. Occasionally, they keep the same mate and return to the very same nest. The nest is built of mud plastered a mouthful at a time on the eave or wall of a building until a cupped half-circle is formed. Before humans built buildings, barn swallows nested in caves and cliff ledges. But once humans came along, the birds seldom went back to their natural nesting spots.

NESTING: Clutch of 5 white-spotted eggs hatches in 13 to 17 days. Nestlings fledge in 18 to 23 days.

PLUMAGE: Iridescent blue above and orange below, with long pointed wings and a deeply forked tail.

SIZE: 7 inches.

CALL: Rapid twitter.

HABITAT: Open country near buildings, including agricultural areas and farmsteads.

STELLER'S JAY
Cyanocitta stelleri

A loud, raucous call precedes a brilliant flash of blue among the pine trees, as the dark-headed Steller's jay works its way through pine trees in its inquisitive, brash manner. It raises its crest when disturbed or agitated—which is often. These residents of western pine forests will cache food and sometimes steal acorns from woodpecker caches. They have an amazing ability to remember where they stored their nuts. Steller's jays feed on acorns, pine seeds, and insects, but may also eat seeds, fruit, and invertebrates.

Like its cousin, the blue jay, the Steller's jay can mimic other birds—especially the scream of the red-tailed hawk! And like their cousins, they are quite mischievous. Steller's jays have earned their nickname "camp robber" by stealing food at many campgrounds. Although some mountain-nesting Steller's jays may migrate to lower elevations, most are resident throughout the year.

Steller's jay; **group:** perching bird; **family:** crow, raven, and jay.

NESTING: Female incubates the 4 blue-green (brown-marked) eggs for 16 days. Fledging time not known, probably 3 weeks.

PLUMAGE: Rich blue body, black barring on wings and tail, and a slate-gray crested head.

SIZE: 12 inches.

CALL: A loud *"shaack! shaack! shaack!"*

HABITAT: Western forests, often near mountains and canyonlands.

BLUE JAY
Cyanocitta cristata

Blue jay; **group:** *perching bird;*
family: *crow, raven, and jay.*

The raucous blue jay is a favorite backyard visitor, but it will often chase away smaller songbirds from feeders. It lives in woodland areas east of the Rockies. The blue jay announces its arrival with its sharp, loud call and a flash of bright blue. Few people know that this bird can mimic other birds—from hawks to songbirds. Blue jays are aggressive birds and often mob crows, hawks, and owls. Blue jays are most often seen in winter when they visit backyard feeders for peanuts, which they relish, sunflower seeds, and cracked corn. In nature, blue jays eat acorns, nuts, seeds, fruit, berries, and insects. They occasionally eat the eggs or nestlings of songbirds.

Many birders argue about blue jays. Some love to have this colorful bird visit their backyard. Others know that a visit from a blue jay can mean a departure, even if for a short time, of smaller songbirds. Even birdwatching can be controversial!

NESTING: Pair builds nest of twigs and grasses in a tree. Clutch of 4 or 5 eggs hatches in 16 to 18 days. Nestlings fledge in 17 to 21 days.

PLUMAGE: Blue overall with black and white markings, gray breast, and prominent blue crest.

A black "necklace" encircles the neck and breast.

SIZE: 11 inches.

CALL: A loud, piercing *"jay, jay, jay."*

HABITAT: Woodlands, suburban parks, and residential areas.

BLACK-BILLED MAGPIE
Pica pica

Black-billed magpie; **group:**
perching bird; **family:** *crow,
raven, and jay.*

The magpie is one of the pirates of the bird world. It seems to like shiny objects, and will steal and bury buttons, pins, and other treasures. This bird is as beautiful as it is mischievous, with its wings and long tail feathers an iridescent green, blue, and amber. Magpies eat almost anything, including insects, small animals such as lizards and mice, carrion, seeds, and fruit. Magpies were considered such pests that up to the 1930s, contests were held to exterminate all magpies.

Magpies form long-term pair bonds. Mates usually stay together all year long. A pair builds a bulky nest of twigs in the shape of a hollow ball. They may take six weeks to build their nest, and they protect their home from thieves by covering it with thorny twigs. Magpies are social and may nest in loose colonies.

NESTING: Female incubates the 5 to 8 green-gray (brown-marked) eggs for about 17 days. Nestlings fledge in 25 to 29 days.

PLUMAGE: Black head, back, and vent with a white belly and wing patches. Wings and tail are iridescent green, blue, and amber.

SIZE: 19 inches.

CALL: A resounding, nasal *"mag?"*

HABITAT: Open western grasslands, sagebrush rangelands, and mountain foothills, especially near water. Occasionally seen on the outskirts of suburban areas.

Black, noisy American crows are aggressive birds that will harass and prey on smaller animals. They will even mob hawks, owls, and other birds of prey. Crows live over most of North America and are social birds that group together. They perform a similar role in nature to gulls—they are nature's garbage collectors. Crows feed on insects, small animals, adult birds, nestlings, other birds' eggs, fruit, seeds, human garbage, and road-killed animals.

The American crow is one of the most intelligent of all birds. Studies show that crows can learn to count to ten, which shows insight learning. They have learned to drop clams in front of passing cars to break them open. Even more amazing, crows have learned to rob ice fishers of their bait. The crow pulls on the line and walks backward with it. Then it walks up to the hole to eat the minnow, but walks on the line so the minnow does not fall back into the water. The crow proves that having a bird brain might not be so bad!

NESTING: Pair incubates the 4 to 6 blue-green or olive-green eggs, which hatch in about 18 days. Nestlings fledge in 4 to 5 weeks.

PLUMAGE: All plumage is black.

SIZE: 17 inches.

CALL: "*Caw-caw.*"

HABITAT: Found in almost every habitat, but are most common near humans.

AMERICAN CROW
Corvus brachyrhynchos

American crow; **group:** *perching bird;* **family:** *crow, raven, and jay.*

The sprightly black-capped chickadee is a common winter visitor to many backyards and rural woodlands. This chickadee is a small, acrobatic bird that nimbly works its way along branches as it looks for food. Black-capped chickadees feed on insects, spiders, and seeds—especially conifer tree seeds. If you want to attract a black-capped chickadee to your backyard, offer it black-oil sunflower seeds and beef suet. Black-capped chickadees do not migrate, instead they form winter flocks that will defend a territory against invaders. Because food during winter is more scarce, they need to ensure that they will have enough food for the flock.

Chickadees build their nests in natural or woodpecker-excavated holes, or in nesting boxes. But they will not often use a nest box unless it is packed with wood chips they can "carve" out to suit their taste. If a female chickadee is disturbed on her nest, she makes a snakelike hiss to warn predators.

NESTING: Pair incubates the 6 to 8 white (red-brown marked) eggs, which hatch in about 12 days. Nestlings fledge in 14 to 17 days.

PLUMAGE: Gray with a distinctive black cap and throat, and a white underside and face.

SIZE: 5 inches.

SONG: Whistled "*fee-bee, fee-bee.*"

HABITAT: Deciduous or mixed-conifer woodlands, forests near water, thickets, and wooded parks.

BLACK-CAPPED CHICKADEE
Parus atricapillus

Black-capped chickadee; **group:** *perching bird;* **family:** *chickadee and titmouse.*

TUFTED TITMOUSE
Parus bicolor

This frequent backyard feeder visitor is related to the chickadee. With its pointed crest, the tufted titmouse is a favorite among suburban residents of the eastern United States. The diet of the tufted titmouse includes insects, spiders, seeds, fruit, and acorns. It is a tame bird that is not afraid to visit a window feeder to get a winter meal of seeds.

Tufted titmice will use nest boxes, especially if they are packed with wood chips so the birds can "carve" out a cavity to suit their tastes. Bird books written around 1900 describe titmice nests as commonly having snakeskins. Today, the birds substitute plastic insulation and cellophane for the hard-to-find snakeskins. Unlike most songbirds, titmice form long-term pair bonds—they mate for life. In fall and winter, they do not migrate. They may form mixed-species flocks with chickadees, nuthatches, and downy woodpeckers.

Tufted titmouse; **group:** perching bird; **family:** chickadee and titmouse.

NESTING: Female incubates the 5 to 7 white spotted eggs about 13 days. Nestlings fledge in 15 to 18 days.

PLUMAGE: Gray above, white below, with rusty-tan flanks. The crest is usually gray, but a Texas race features a black tuft.

SIZE: 7 inches.

SONG: *"Peter, peter, peter."*

HABITAT: Woodlands, parklands, and residential areas.

Few birds climb trees, but the white-breasted nuthatch prefers to climb down trees—seemingly upside down and head first. Its feet and claws allow the nuthatch to cling to tree trunks and branches as it searches for insects and larvae, picking into the bark's crevices to find hidden food. Its movements are jerky as it moves in spurts, periodically calling a nasal *"yank-yank"* or taking flight to another tree to continue spiraling down the trunk. During the winter nuthatches often eat nuts and seeds, as their name implies.

During the breeding season, you may see one adult nuthatch feeding another adult. This is called "courtship feeding." Males feed their mates, which is soon followed by copulation. Courtship feeding helps the birds to pair bond, may reduce aggression, or may be the male's way of ensuring the female (carrying his eggs) is well nourished.

WHITE-BREASTED NUTHATCH
Sitta carolinensis

White-breasted nuthatch; **group:** perching bird; **family:** nuthatch.

NESTING: Female incubates the 5 to 8 white (red-brown marked) eggs about 12 days. Nestlings fledge in about 2 weeks.

PLUMAGE: Black cap, white face and breast, pale-blue back, and bluish wings and tail, which are marked with black and white.

SIZE: 6 inches.

CALL: *"Yank-yank."*

HABITAT: Woodlands, and small woodlots.

The bubbling, lively song of the little house wren is a favorite for city dwellers throughout the United States and southern Canada. This sassy backyard nester has a habit of tipping its tail straight up. This is especially endearing when it makes its way in its hurried, jerking fashion as it searches for insects and spiders.

House wrens nest in cavities, usually a woodpecker hole, a natural site, or a nest box. Sometimes a pair selects an unusual location like a crevice in a wall or an open mailbox. Males build the nests of small twigs, grass, and feathers. House wrens may nest twice and sometimes three times.

House wrens cause headaches for people maintaining trails of bluebird nest boxes. Male house wrens build many "dummy nests"—only one of which is finally selected and used. So bluebirds lose those potential nesting sites. And both house wren parents destroy the eggs of other cavity nesters nearby.

HOUSE WREN
Troglodytes aedon

House wren; **group:** *perching bird;* **family:** *wren.*

NESTING: Female incubates the 6 to 8 white (brown-marked) eggs for 13 days. Nestlings fledge in 12 to 18 days.

PLUMAGE: Medium brown with black markings above and a tan underside.

SIZE: 5 inches.

SONG: A bubbling high-pitched series of notes.

HABITAT: Brushy woodlands and orchards, and shrubby backyards and parks.

EASTERN BLUEBIRD
Sialia sialis

Eastern bluebird; **group:** *perching bird;* **family:** *thrush.*

One of the sure signs of spring in many areas of eastern North America is the return of the eastern bluebird—the darling of North American birders. It is a much-loved bird that many birders try to attract to their yards with nest boxes. Many concerned birders have built and continue to watch bluebird nest-box trails to encourage bluebirds to nest and reproduce. The bluebird has been a victim of more aggressive, introduced birds, such as European starlings and house sparrows.

If you live within the eastern bluebird's range, you can try to attract them to your area by building nest boxes. Make sure the entrance hole is exactly 1½ inches—that allows bluebirds in but not bigger birds such as starlings.

NESTING: Female incubates the 4 or 5 pale-blue eggs, which hatch in 12 to 14 days. Nestlings fledge in 10 to 16 days.

PLUMAGE: Male has a bright blue head, back, wings, and tail; a bright orange chin and breast; and a white belly and vent. Females are similar, but duller.

SIZE: 7 inches.

SONG: An extended *"chur-churlee-churlee."*

HABITAT: Open country with scattered trees or woodland edges. Also agricultural areas near tree belts and rural homes.

AMERICAN ROBIN
Turdus migratorius

The male American robin's beautiful spring song promises respite from the cold weather of winter. The American robin is a hardy bird; it lives in cities as well as in the country. This thrush feeds on earthworms, insects, berries, and fruit. If you've ever watched a robin searching for worms, you've seen it cock its head as if it were listening for the worm's movements in the earth. But ornithologists have proven that robins locate worms by sight.

The American robin was the inspiration for the title of Rachel Carson's famous book, *Silent Spring*. The silent spring referred to a spring without the robin's song. During the 1950s, DDT was used extensively to kill the beetles that spread Dutch elm disease. The DDT coated the elm leaves, which were eaten by worms, which were eaten by robins, which were poisoned and died. So the American robin started the environmental movement—with help from Rachel Carson!

NESTING: Female incubates the 4 "robin's-egg-blue" eggs, which hatch in 12 to 14 days. Nestlings fledge in about 2 weeks.

PLUMAGE: Males have a gray-brown back, a black head, and a bright orange breast. The female's plumage is duller; male resembles female during nonbreeding season.

SIZE: 10 inches.

SONG: A variable *"cheery-cheery-cheerio-cheery-cheriup-cheery."*

HABITAT: From forests to open woodland edges to residential areas.

American robin; **group:** *perching bird;* **family:** *thrush.*

NORTHERN MOCKINGBIRD
Mimus polyglottos

The northern mockingbird is one of the singing champions of the continent. Few birds can rival the beautiful, spirited songs it sings. The mockingbird can mimic the songs of other birds, but it also has its own songs. And this bird can even imitate a barking dog, squeaky gate, or meowing cat! Its scientific name is very appropriate, "mimic of many tongues." Unmated males sing more than males with mates. In fact, it is the unmated males who keep the neighborhood up as they sing throughout the night. A female picks a male that has the largest repertory of songs for her mate. Northern mockingbirds feed on insects, spiders, and fruit.

But don't be fooled by the northern mockingbird's song. Just because it can make beautiful music, doesn't mean it is a gentle bird. It will aggressively defend its nesting territory.

NESTING: Female incubates the 3 to 5 blue-green (brown-marked) eggs for 12 to 13 days. Nestlings fledge in 11 to 13 days.

PLUMAGE: Light gray above, black wings and tail, white underside, wing patches, and outer tail feathers.

SIZE: 10 inches.

SONG: A melodic variety of imitated and original songs.

HABITAT: A variety of open habitats including suburban backyards.

Northern mockingbird; **group:** *perching bird;* **family:** *mimic thrush.*

CEDAR WAXWING
Bombycilla cedrorum

On a quiet winter day, as snow falls on a leafless crab apple tree, a colorful flock flies in to dine on the soft fruit that still hangs from the bare branches. The smooth tan plumage of the cedar waxwing is set off by its black mask and hoodlike crest. The flock mobs the tree, as 100 or more birds quickly grab the rotted soft fruit, dropping as many crab apples as they swallow. They are a colorful flurry of feeding activity. Flocks move from food source to food source after the breeding season. Fruit is their favorite food, but they feed their nestlings insects for the first few weeks. Growing nestlings need more protein than fruit can provide.

Waxwings can often be spotted lined up in a row, passing a berry up and down the line before one bird finally eats the berry. And a breeding pair will often pass flower petals back and forth to each other. If Shakespeare had seen that, there surely would be a sonnet about waxwing courtship!

Cedar waxwing; **group:** *perching bird;* **family:** *waxwing.*

NESTING: Female incubates the 5 pale blue-gray spotted eggs for 12 days. Nestlings fledge in about 15 days.

PLUMAGE: A black facial mask and sharp crest are distinctive. Both sexes have a tan head, breast, and back; yellow belly and tail stripe; and gray wings, rump, and tail. They have red tips on the end of their secondary feathers.

SIZE: 7 inches.

CALL: A soft, high-pitched trill.

HABITAT: Woodlands, forested river valleys, and suburban areas.

EUROPEAN STARLING
Sturnus vulgaris

While many bird species have been reduced in numbers over the past century, the European starling has spread throughout most of North America since it was introduced to the streets of New York City 100 years ago. They spread from the East to the Pacific Coast in only 60 years!

In 1890, the American Acclimatization Society thought that every bird mentioned in Shakespeare's plays should live in America. The first two attempts to introduce starlings failed—but the third was very successful. Since then, North American birds and people have suffered! In fact, this species has been partly responsible for reducing populations of bluebirds and other cavity-nesting birds. Starlings are aggressive and take over many possible nesting sites. They feed on insects, seeds, fruits, and berries. But not everyone has thought of starlings as pests. Starlings have such lovely vocal ability that Mozart kept one as a pet!

European starling; **group:** *perching bird;* **family:** *starling.*

NESTING: Pair incubates the 4 to 6 eggs for 12 to 14 days. Nestlings fledge in 18 to 21 days.

PLUMAGE: Iridescent black and brown with white or yellow feather tips.

SIZE: 8 inches.

CALL: A variety of squeaky notes and warbling phrases; starlings can also imitate other birds.

HABITAT: Open woodlands, farmsteads, and urban areas.

YELLOW WARBLER
Dendroica petechia

Yellow warbler; **group:** *perching bird;* **family:** *New World warbler.*

Yellow warblers are one of the most beautiful songbirds. They are often found in fields and can possibly be found in your backyard. Sometimes confused with goldfinches, yellow warblers are members of the wood warbler family. Like most warblers, the yellow species feeds mainly on small insects and spiders it gleans from tree leaves.

Female yellow warblers build a bowl-shaped nest by weaving grass and weeds. Cowbirds often leave their eggs in yellow warbler nests. But the yellow warbler knows how to deal with the cowbird eggs. If she has not yet laid her eggs, or laid only one, she will rebuild her nest over the old one. But if she has laid her full clutch of 4 or 5 eggs, then she accepts the cowbird egg and incubates it. It may be that because the warblers have a head start on growing, the warbler young are not in as much danger from the larger cowbird nestling.

NESTING: Female builds nest and incubates the 4 or 5 white spotted eggs about 11 days. Nestlings fledge in 12 days.

PLUMAGE: The male is bright yellow with orange-red streaks on its breast. Females are lighter yellow overall and may lack the streaked breast feathers.

SIZE: 5 inches.

SONG: Six-syllable song, *"sweet, sweet, sweet, I'm so sweet."*

HABITAT: Willow thickets and open woodlands; residential areas, parks, and orchards in east.

A flock of twittering small birds moves through a stand of trees, working the bottoms of leaves with their short, pointed bills looking for small caterpillars, insects, and spiders. Yellow-rumped warblers flit from leaf to leaf, branch to branch, occasionally showing their yellow rump patch.

John James Audubon, one of the first bird artists and one of the fathers of American ornithology, originally had three birds named in his honor. But modern classification has stripped him of two of the three birds; the yellow-rumped warbler was one of them. Audubon's warbler was reclassified as the yellow-rumped warbler. Audubon's oriole was reclassified as the black-headed oriole. The only bird remaining that bears his name is the Audubon's shearwater.

NESTING: Female incubates the 4 or 5 white spotted eggs for 12 days. Nestlings fledge in 10 to 12 days.

PLUMAGE: Male is blue gray above; yellow cap, rump, and sides of breast; black breast and sides. Female is duller.

SIZE: 5 inches.

SONG: A musical *"weetie, weetie, weeteo."*

HABITAT: Pine forests and mixed woodlands.

YELLOW-RUMPED WARBLER
Dendroica coronata

Yellow-rumped warbler; **group:** *perching bird;* **family:** *New World warbler.*

NORTHERN CARDINAL
Cardinalis cardinalis

This gaudy red-crested bird is one of the favorite backyard birds in the eastern United States. The bright crimson male is one of the easiest American birds to identify. The female is no less beautiful with buff-tan plumage highlighted by red. A pair of cardinals provides an exciting sight, even for veteran backyard birders. Northern cardinals eat insects, seeds, and fruit. They have thick, conical bills that are well suited for cracking seeds. They flock to backyard feeding stations and prefer black-oil sunflower and safflower seeds.

The cardinal is one of the few North American species in which the female sings. After a breeding pair has established their territory, they engage in countersinging where the male sings, and the female imitates. This probably strengthens their pair bond and gets them ready to mate.

*Northern cardinal; **group:** perching bird; **family:** sparrow and finch.*

NESTING: Female builds nest of plant stems, twigs, and bark while male sings. Both incubate the 3 or 4 gray, pale-green, or pale-blue eggs, which hatch in about 12 days. Nestlings fledge in about 10 days.

PLUMAGE: Males have bright red bodies with a black face and throat. Females have tan bodies that are bordered by red; the wings, tail, and crest are light red. Immature cardinals resemble the female. All have a pronounced crest and long tail.

SIZE: 8¾ inches.

SONG: Repetition of loud slurred whistles of 5 to 10 minutes long.

HABITAT: Open forests, woodland edges, and residential areas.

A flock of large finches descends on a backyard feeder; their appetite for seeds seems huge compared to other winter visitors. This flock of evening grosbeaks adds flashes of yellow and brown to the scene. The grosbeaks take over during their stay; their numbers and activity are too much for the other birds. Once the grosbeaks have eaten their fill, they fly away and the feeder becomes quieter with the return of chickadees, nuthatches, and cardinals. Evening grosbeaks feed on seeds, juniper berries, tree buds, and insects.

Evening grosbeaks are very tame and are often found around where people live. This unfortunately can work against them. They will eat road salt, and so in winter they are frequently killed by cars.

NESTING: Female incubates the 3 or 4 blue or blue-green spotted eggs for 11 to 14 days. Nestlings fledge in 2 weeks.

PLUMAGE: The male is brown and yellow, with a prominent yellow brow and eye stripe, and a black cap. The female is gray brown overall. Both sexes have black tails and wings, with white wing patches.

SIZE: 8 inches.

CALL: Sharp "*peeir.*"

HABITAT: Evergreen and mixed woodlands and mountain forests for breeding.

EVENING GROSBEAK
Coccothraustes vespertinus

*Evening grosbeak; **group:** perching bird; **family:** sparrow and finch.*

With such a pretty name, you might expect these birds to be lovely. And you would not be disappointed. Male indigo buntings are beautiful birds. The indigo bunting is the most commonly found species of buntings. The male is a rich indigo blue. It is most often found singing with its head held high, on an exposed bush on the shrubby border of a stream. Buntings belong to the larger group of finchlike birds that also includes sparrows, cardinals, and grosbeaks. Indigo buntings eat insects, seeds, and berries.

While the songs of indigo buntings may sound alike to humans, the songs are very different. Their song patterns declare their territory, and the birds know the songs of their neighbors. If an unfamiliar indigo bunting were to enter an area, the "neighborhood" would know by its different song. Some young birds imitate the song of an older bird so it can share that bird's territory.

NESTING: Female incubates the 3 or 4 pale-blue or white eggs, which hatch in about 12 days. Nestlings fledge in 9 days.

PLUMAGE: The male is a deep blue during breeding season, but molts to a medium brown with a tan underside and a sexually distinct blue rump in winter. The female is medium brown.

SIZE: 5 inches.

SONG: High-pitched *"quick, quick, help, help, fire, fire!"*

HABITAT: Brushy areas and woodland borders.

INDIGO BUNTING
Passerina cyanea

*Indigo bunting; **group:** perching bird; **family:** sparrow and finch.*

PAINTED BUNTING

Passerina ciris

*Painted bunting; **group:** perching bird; **family:** sparrow and finch.*

Sporting bright patches of blue, red, green, and brown, the male painted bunting is one of the most colorful of all North American birds. The gaudy-colored males keep their intense colors all year. Females look very different, with bright green above and yellow green below—but they are also quite lovely. A nesting pair of painted buntings is an impressive sight. A Native American legend says that when the Great Spirit was handing out colors for birds, he ran out of dye. So he gave the very last he had to the painted bunting—dabs of different colors! These buntings feed chiefly on seeds, but also prey on insects and spiders.

Though many colors on a bird appear because of pigment, the blue you see on the painted bunting—and every other blue bird—is not a pigment. It is actually an optical illusion. It appears blue because of the way the light is scattered by the feathers and then reflected.

NESTING: Female incubates the 3 or 4 blue-white (brown-spotted) eggs about 11 days. Nestlings fledge in 12 to 14 days.

PLUMAGE: The male has a blue head, green back, red breast and rump, and brown wings and tail.

SIZE: 5 inches.

SONG: A rapid, high-pitched warbling.

HABITAT: Brushy areas, woodland borders, and river thickets.

SONG SPARROW
Melospiza melodia

Song sparrow; **group:** perching bird; **family:** sparrow and finch.

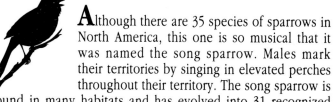

Although there are 35 species of sparrows in North America, this one is so musical that it was named the song sparrow. Males mark their territories by singing in elevated perches throughout their territory. The song sparrow is found in many habitats and has evolved into 31 recognized subspecies, which can be distinguished by physical and musical differences. Various races can sing over 20 different melodies and can improvise hundreds of variations on those songs! Song sparrows feed on insects, seeds, grains, and sometimes berries.

The male song sparrow will sing through breeding season, into summer, fall, and even winter. The female will join him before nesting, but her song is softer and shorter than the male's. These birds begin practicing singing very early—as they learn to fly.

NESTING: Female incubates the 3 or 4 pale-blue or green spotted eggs for 12 to 14 days. Nestlings fledge in 9 to 12 days.

PLUMAGE: Most are medium brown with spotting on their back, a light breast with streaking, and a distinctive spot in the center of their breast.

SIZE: 6 inches.

SONG: A beautiful, melodic song: "*Maids, maids, maids, put on the tea kettle, ettle, ettle.*"

HABITAT: Variable habitats, often in dense vegetation bordering marshes, rivers, forest edges, or gardens.

WHITE-CROWNED SPARROW
Zonotrichia leucophrys

Many sparrows are shy, retiring birds. The species are hard to tell apart because they look alike and are so secretive. But the white-crowned sparrow is very distinctive, with its black- and white-striped cap. It often perches with its body held upright, as if it knew it were wearing a crown and should act kingly (or queenly). It is also a rather large sparrow, about one to one and a half inches longer than its cousin the song sparrow.

Though the white-crowned sparrow does not stand a chance against the virtuoso performance of the song sparrow, its clear, whistled song is certainly lovely and quite a good diversion on a winter's day. You can try to entice it to your backyard by providing seeds. The white-crowned sparrow eats insects, seeds, and grain. It may even repay you with a song if you offer white millet or black-oil sunflower seeds.

NESTING: Female builds nest and incubates the 3 to 5 pale-blue (rust-spotted) eggs for 12 days. Nestlings fledge in about 10 days.

PLUMAGE: Brown-streaked back, light gray undersides, and black- and white-striped head. Bill is pink.

SIZE: 7 inches.

SONG: Clear whistles, followed by buzzy whistles.

HABITAT: Edges of woodlands, northern spruce forests, and brushy thickets.

White-crowned sparrow; **group:** perching bird; **family:** sparrow and finch.

DARK-EYED JUNCO
Junco hyemalis

*Dark-eyed junco; **group:** perching bird; **family:** sparrow and finch.*

The dark-eyed junco is the most common visitor to winter bird feeders throughout most of North America. It is a social bird during the winter, but mated birds go their separate ways during nesting season. Ornithologists once thought the four races were separate species (slate-colored, Oregon, gray-headed, and white-winged), but now they are considered the same species. Dark-eyed juncos feed on seeds and insects. At backyard feeders, juncos prefer white proso millet and cracked corn—especially when offered on the ground.

Males and females take separate vacations. The males are larger and can handle cold weather better. So they winter farther north than the smaller females.

NESTING: Female incubates the 3 to 5 eggs for 12 to 13 days. Nestlings fledge in 9 to 13 days.

PLUMAGE: Colors differ between races. The slate-colored race is slate gray with a white belly. The Oregon race has a black head and breast, dark-gray wings, light-brown back and sides, white belly, and gray rump. The gray-headed race is gray with a brown back. The white-winged race resembles slate-colored birds, with lighter gray overall and two white wing stripes. Females are lighter colored overall. All races have a gray tail with broad white borders and yellow beak and legs.

SIZE: 6 inches.

CALL: A sharp "*sleep.*"

HABITAT: Forested mountains, open woodlands, and well-planted suburban areas.

RED-WINGED BLACKBIRD
Agelaius phoeniceus

*Red-winged blackbird; **group:** perching bird; **family:** oriole and blackbird.*

Perched on a cattail, a territorial male red-winged blackbird spreads its wings to show off its red upper-wing patches (called epaulets) and it gives its loud, squeaky three-syllable call. Across the marsh, other male red-wings answer the call. These calls echo throughout the marsh. Red-winged blackbirds feed on seeds, grains, insects, and spiders.

In spring, the older males return north first, staking out their territory. The females follow and there is a flurry of activity while males try to entice females to mate with them. Red-winged blackbirds are polygynous, that is, one male will breed with one or more females. Once that activity has settled down, the young males returning north stir up everything again. But the females have already nested and the older males are not giving up any territory.

NESTING: Female incubates the 3 or 4 pale blue-green eggs for 10 to 12 days. Nestlings fledge within 2 weeks.

PLUMAGE: Males are deep black with red upper-wing patches with yellow lower border. Females are brown above, streaked white and brown below, often with pink wash on head and throat.

SIZE: 9 inches.

SONG: "*Konk-la-ree*" or "*book-rrr-tee.*"

HABITAT: Shallow wetlands, grasslands, and hayfields, brushy woodlands, and agricultural fields.

A prairie marsh is alive with the songs and displays of blackbirds with bright-yellow heads. Appropriately named, these male yellow-headed blackbirds are spaced out on territories throughout the cattails and reeds surrounding the wetland. Each male takes his turn flashing his white wing patches. He raises his head toward the sky to sing in response to his neighbor's calls. To gain the attention of a female, he bows in a courtly gesture and begins to sing. But only a female yellow-headed blackbird would appreciate his song. It may be one of the most unmusical of all songbirds!

Yellow-headed blackbirds are found in the vegetation of wetlands during breeding season. Yellow-headed blackbirds prefer deeper wetlands than its cousin, the red-winged blackbird. They feed on insects, snails, and seeds, including agricultural grains and sunflowers.

NESTING: Female incubates the 4 pale-green (brown- and gray-marked) eggs about 13 days. Nestlings fledge in 9 to 12 days.

PLUMAGE: Black overall, except the male has a white wing patch and a bright-yellow head and breast; females have less yellow on the head and a duller breast.

SIZE: 9 inches.

SONG: A raspy note that ends in a descending buzz.

HABITAT: Vegetation surrounding freshwater wetlands, farmlands, and tree groves.

YELLOW-HEADED BLACKBIRD
Xanthocephalus xanthocephalus

Yellow-headed blackbird; **group:** *perching bird;* **family:** *oriole and blackbird.*

The popularity of the western meadowlark is perhaps best underscored by the fact that six states (Kansas, Montana, Nebraska, North Dakota, Oregon, and Wyoming) have claimed this melodic grassland bird as their state bird. The beautiful call of the male western meadowlark is one of the first signs of spring in the northern part of its breeding range. Its bright yellow breast with black "necklace" makes it an easy bird to identify. Meadowlarks are members of the blackbird family. Meadowlarks eat mostly insects and spiders, but they also eat grain and seeds.

The western meadowlark is nearly identical to the eastern meadowlark. The best way to tell them apart is by their song. Ornithologists call them "sibling species." They are species that are extremely similar in appearance but do not interbreed.

NESTING: Pair incubates the 3 to 6 eggs about 2 weeks. Nestlings fledge in 11 or 12 days.

PLUMAGE: Tan mottled with white and black on the back, yellow throat and belly, black chest band, and white- and brown-striped head.

SIZE: 10 inches.

SONG: A melodious gurgling and double-noted song.

HABITAT: Grasslands and agricultural fields.

WESTERN MEADOWLARK
Sturnella neglecta

Western meadowlark; **group:** *perching bird;* **family:** *oriole and blackbird.*

COMMON GRACKLE
Quiscalus quiscula

*Common grackle; **group:** perching bird; **family:** oriole and blackbird.*

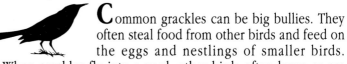

Common grackles can be big bullies. They often steal food from other birds and feed on the eggs and nestlings of smaller birds. When grackles fly into a yard, other birds often leave or are chased away. Grackles feed on a variety of foods, but they mostly eat insects and seeds.

Common grackles usually nest in loose colonies. In fall, large flocks can number in the hundreds of thousands, and can damage farm crops. In winter, they form roosts with starlings and other blackbirds that can number up to several million birds! The song of the common grackle is not beautiful—it sounds more like a rusty gate squeaking. Imagine what a flock of 100,000 birds sounds like—a bit overwhelming!

Grackles are one of the causes of the decline of eastern songbirds. Humans have divided eastern forests so much that grackles and other nest predators can reach songbird nests and destroy their eggs and/or young. But don't blame the birds—humans created the situation!

NESTING: Female builds nest and incubates the 4 or 5 greenish-white or light-brown (brown- or purple-marked) eggs about 2 weeks. Nestlings fledge in 16 to 20 days.

PLUMAGE: Iridescent black. The female has a shorter tail and is not as shiny.

SIZE: 12 inches.

SONG: A squeaky "*kubalee-eek.*"

HABITAT: Open fields, farmlands, and suburban areas.

The scarlet tanager is a songbird that is as beautiful as its name. The male is spectacularly colored during breeding season, with a crimson body and black wings and tail feathers. These lovely birds feed mostly on insects, but they also eat berries.

Unfortunately, this bird is in danger. Scarlet tanagers travel to Central and South America for the winter. But because of the large-scale destruction of rain forests, their winter areas are becoming much smaller. And in North America, their breeding range is also growing smaller because of development for homes, shopping malls, and other signs of civilization. But the female tanager does fight one threat to her species. Cowbirds often leave their eggs in a tanager nest. The cowbird nestling survives but often the tanager nestlings do not. Female tanagers recognize female cowbirds and drive them away.

SCARLET TANAGER
Piranga olivacea

*Scarlet tanager; **group:** perching bird; **family:** sparrow and finch.*

NESTING: Female incubates the 2 to 5 blue or green (brown-spotted) eggs, which hatch after 13 days. Nestlings fledge in 10 days.

PLUMAGE: Females, nonbreeding males, and immature scarlet tanagers have olive backs and wings and yellow undersides. Breeding males have bright crimson bodies with black wing and tail feathers.

SIZE: 7 inches.

SONG: A robinlike song—"*kwerit, kweer, kwery.*"

HABITAT: Mixed deciduous-conifer forests and woodlands.

A brilliant flicker of a red-headed, golden-yellow bird with black wings—steered in flight by its black tail—brightens an open glade in a mountain pine forest. Few western birds can rival the male western tanager for its startling beauty. So different from her mate, the female looks like a different species with an olive back, yellow belly, and slate-gray wings. But after the breeding season, the gaudy male molts into a plumage similar to the female. The western tanager is the western counterpart of the scarlet tanager, which nests in the eastern part of the United States.

Western tanagers feed on insects and some fruit and berries. They migrate south from their breeding range to Central America where insects are still plentiful during winter.

NESTING: Female incubates the 3 to 5 bluish (brown-marked) eggs about 13 days. Nestlings fledge in less than 2 weeks.

PLUMAGE: Breeding male has red head, yellow body, black tail and wings, with two yellow wing bars. During winter, males resemble the females, which are yellow below and olive above with gray wings and tail.

SIZE: 7 inches.

SONG: Sounds like a hoarse robin with a pause after each phrase.

HABITAT: Coniferous mountain forests.

WESTERN TANAGER
Piranga ludoviciana

*Western tanager; **group:** perching bird; **family:** sparrow and finch.*

BROWN-HEADED COWBIRD

Molothrus ater

*Brown-headed cowbird; **group:** perching bird; **family:** oriole and blackbird.*

B rown-headed cowbirds have the most unusual nesting behavior of any North American bird. They do not build nests, do not incubate their eggs, and do not care for their young. Yet they successfully breed. How? The female cowbird lays its eggs in the nests of other songbirds. Cowbirds are brood parasites that rely on other birds to incubate their eggs.

Incubation by the host bird takes about 12 days and the cowbird young fledge in about 10 days. The young cowbirds are usually larger than the other nestlings and develop quicker than their foster siblings. They eat more than their share of food brought by the host adults. The cowbirds' nesting behavior is harmful for the foster species—usually warblers, vireos, and other small songbirds. (Cowbird eggs have been found in over 220 species' nests!) But some bird species will not raise the cowbird young. Some birds recognize cowbird eggs and desert the nest or destroy the cowbird eggs.

NESTING: Female leaves eggs in other birds' nests.

PLUMAGE: Males are metallic blue-black with a dull-brown head. Females are medium brown.

SIZE: 7 inches.

CALL: Squeaky gurgling notes and whistles.

HABITAT: Farmlands, grasslands, suburban areas, and open woodlands.

NORTHERN ORIOLE
Icterus galbula

The northern oriole is one of America's favorite songbirds. Aside from its song, it is also well known for its lovely coloring and its pouch-shaped, hanging woven nest. The northern oriole was named when ornithologists realized that Baltimore and Bullock's orioles are the same species. Northern orioles feed on insects, fruit, and flower nectar.

The northern oriole's nest is a masterwork of engineering and art. The female builds the hanging nest, which is made of stem fibers that are woven into a basketlike pouch. Though it may look a bit precarious, it has served the northern oriole population well. Since the clutch size is 4 or 5 eggs, that means that 4 or 5 chicks, if all survive, are brooded in the nest. And bird young are not known for staying still!

NESTING: Female incubates the 4 or 5 eggs, which hatch in 12 to 14 days. Nestlings fledge in less than 2 weeks.

PLUMAGE: Baltimore males have a black head, throat, back, tail, and wings and an orange belly, vent, rump, and tail patches. Bullock's males are a lighter orange, with an orange face, black eye stripe, and large white wing patches. Female Baltimore orioles are brown above and light orange below; female Bullock's orioles are mostly olive.

SIZE: 8¾ inches.

SONG: A varied, musical series of notes.

HABITAT: Open woodlands, edges of deciduous forests; open areas with scattered trees; and backyards.

Northern oriole; **group:** *perching bird;* **family:** *oriole and blackbird.*

HOUSE FINCH
Carpodacus mexicanus

For such a small bird, the male house finch can sing a powerfully beautiful song. While this finch is native to the western United States, it has expanded across most of the country. House finches were being sold in pet shops as "Hollywood finches," which was a violation of federal law. When word got out that the authorities were going to check pet shops, the owners in the New York City area released the birds rather than facing arrest. The birds established a population on Long Island in 1941 and have undergone explosive population growth.

It appears that eastern populations will soon meet western finches. Though these are melodic birds, not everyone is happy to see them prosper. As house finches increase in an area, house sparrows and purple finches decline.

NESTING: Female builds nest and incubates the 4 or 5 light-blue or light blue-green spotted eggs for 12 to 14 days. Nestlings fledge in 11 to 19 days.

PLUMAGE: Mostly brown with a lighter breast streaked with brown. Males have a bright-red breast, throat, face, and rump. In rare cases, the red is replaced by yellow or orange.

SIZE: 6 inches.

SONG: A multisyllabic, melodic song.

HABITAT: Suburbs, farmlands, and dry open areas with thickets and scrubs.

House finch; **group:** *perching bird;* **family:** *sparrow and finch.*

AMERICAN GOLDFINCH
Carduelis tristis

*American goldfinch; **group:** perching bird; **family:** sparrow and finch.*

The American goldfinch provides a spectacular flash of yellow in the open fields and meadows where it lives. The goldfinch is a common bird and one of America's favorite backyard birds—you can try attracting it by putting up a feeder with thistle or black-oil sunflower seeds. In the wild, they eat plant and tree seeds.

The American goldfinch is one of the last birds to migrate north in spring, and one of the last birds to begin nesting. American goldfinches delay nesting until the thistle blooms in late summer. Thistle down is used to line their nests, and the seeds are regurgitated and fed to the young. The female weaves a tight, bowl-shaped nest of dried plants in the fork of a tree branch. This bird's nest is so tightly woven that it will fill with water in a rainstorm and drown the nestlings unless a parent is there to shield the nestlings with its wings. Some American goldfinches nest twice in a breeding season.

NESTING: Female incubates the 4 to 6 pale-blue eggs for 10 to 12 days. Nestlings fledge in 11 to 17 days.

PLUMAGE: The male is bright yellow with a black cap, wings, and tail during breeding season; males molt to resemble females during winter. Females are duller, with an olive back and no cap.

SIZE: 5 inches.

SONG: A series of canarylike trills.

HABITAT: Open fields with thistles, sunflowers, and other "weeds," usually near water.

HOUSE SPARROW
Passer domesticus

*House sparrow; **group:** perching bird; **family:** weaver finch.*

House sparrows were introduced to the United States between 1850 and 1867 because people thought they were attractive and would help control insect pests. In only 50 years, this common urban and farmyard resident spread throughout the entire United States. The house sparrow is common in inner-city streets where you might catch a male hopping in front of a female with its wings held low to the ground in its courtship display. House sparrows feed mostly on seeds but eat some insects and spiders; city birds eat almost anything.

In the early 1900s, house sparrows were the most abundant bird in North America. Their populations declined with the invention of the automobile. Not only did grain disappear with more urban centers, but much of the horse manure, a major food source, disappeared.

House sparrow nests have been found at the bottom of the large stick nests of hawks. Their large and fierce neighbors defend both nests from predators. Not a bad neighbor to have!

NESTING: Female incubates the 4 to 6 eggs for 10 to 13 days. Nestlings fledge in 14 to 17 days.

PLUMAGE: The male is mostly chestnut-brown with a gray cap, cheeks, and belly, and a black bib. The female is mostly brown above and light gray below.

SIZE: 6 inches.

CALL: Repeated "*chirps.*"

HABITAT: Near human dwellings.

GLOSSARY

Adaptions   Changes that happen over a long time—maybe millions of years—that help an organism survive.

Altricial   Newly hatched nestlings that are helpless. They are usually blind, have no feathers, cannot regulate their body temperatures, and need constant care and feeding by the parent birds.

Brood   A family of nestlings. As a verb, it is what the parent birds do when they take care of the young.

Carrion   The remains of dead animals.

Cavity nester   A bird that must nest in a cavity, such as in a hollowed-out hole in a tree. A nest box is an artificial hole made by humans to encourage cavity-nesting birds to nest.

Clutch   A complete set of eggs. Some birds lay more than one clutch each year.

Creche   A place where an adult "guardian" watches the colony's chicks so the parent birds can go out and find food for their young. Greater flamingos, royal and sandwich terns, eiders, ostriches, and some gulls and penguins form creches.

Crest   A pointed tuft of feathers on the head of a bird, such as a northern cardinal.

Crop   A thin-walled, saclike food storage chamber that projects outward from the bottom of the esophagus. Large crops permit birds to gather and store food quickly, minimizing the time exposed to predators. Crops are well developed in pigeons, gamebirds, and raptors.

Cryptic coloring   The camouflage coloring on a bird that conceals it in its habitat.

Cygnet   A newly hatched swan.

Eclipse plumage   After nesting season, most male ducks molt their brightly colored breeding plumage into a dull, camouflaged plumage—called eclipse plumage. The change occurs quickly but for a brief time leaves the drakes flightless.

Endangered species   A species that is so rare that it will become extinct in the near future.

Extinct   A species that is no longer living, like dinosaurs and passenger pigeons.

Fledge   To fly, usually from the nest, for the first time.

Fledgling   A young bird that has grown enough feathers to be able to fly.

Flock   A group of birds that stay together for protection, to find food, or to migrate.

Genus   Closely related species are grouped together into a genus.

Habitat   Where an animal lives; the special kind of environment it needs to survive.

Hybrid   The offspring of two animals or plants of different species.

Incubate   To keep eggs warm so they will hatch. An incubating bird sits on the eggs, warming them with its body heat.

Invertebrates   Animals that do not have a spinal column, such as shrimp, insects, and clams.

Iridescence   Iridescent colors are produced by the way light reflects off the surface of the feathers. Unlike most colors in birds (except blue), iridescent colors are not created by pigment.

Lek   A place where male birds gather to display and perform their courtship dances, in hopes of attracting a female. (Lek is the Swedish word for play.)

Molt   To replace old feathers and grow new ones.

Nest   The place where a bird lays its eggs. As a verb, it is the act of building or occupying a nest.

Nestling   A chick, from the time it hatches to the time it fledges.

Ornithologist   A scientist who studies birds.

Ornithology   The scientific study of birds.

Plumage   A bird's feathers.

Precocial   Newly hatched chicks that are covered with down and can walk and feed themselves hours after hatching.

Predator   Any animal—including birds—that catches, kills, and eats other animals.

Prey   The animals that are eaten by predators.

Primary feathers   The outermost flight feathers on birds' wings. Also called primaries.

Range   The area over which a species of bird is found. Bird ranges constantly expand and contract.

Raptors   Birds of prey. This group includes eagles, falcons, vultures, and hawks.

Roost   The place where a bird spends the night; a "roost hole" is a hole where a bird spends the night, or where it takes shelter in bad weather.

Scrape   A bare, scratched out hollow on the ground where some birds build their nests. They sometimes lay plants or feathers on top of the ground in the scrape.

Scavenger   An animal or bird that feeds on dead or discarded things, rather than catching live prey.

Secondary feathers   The innermost flight feathers on a bird's wing. Also called secondaries.

Species   A group of closely related living things that are much alike and that can breed with one another, producing viable offspring, in the wild.

Speculum   A patch of color on the secondaries of most ducks and some other birds. Plural of speculum is specula.

Wingspan   The distance from one wing tip to the other, when a bird has its wings fully spread.

INDEX